Carolina Folk Plays

2020

Carolina Folk Plays

2020

Four one-act plays
by students from
The University of North Carolina
at Chapel Hill

With an Introduction by
Mark Perry

DRAMA CIRCLE
Chapel Hill, North Carolina

Drama Circle
P.O. Box 3844
Chapel Hill, NC 27515 USA

Email: info@dramacircle.org
Website: www.dramacircle.org

Cover Art by Cole Kordus

The plays contained in this volume remain the intellectual property of their respective writers. They may be available for your group to produce. Contact the publisher for contact information and to apply for permission. No performance may be given without written permission.

Carolina Folk Plays: 2020 Edition
    Copyright © 2020 by Cole Kordus, Emily Jane MacKillop, Sorcha de Faoite, Sam Bible-Sullivan, and Mark E. Perry.
ISBN: 978-0-9834701-9-9
Library of Congress Control Number: 2020941395

20 21 22 23 24 25   10 9 8 7 6 5 4 3 2 1

TABLE OF CONTENTS

"Time worn walls give back their echo"

Revisiting the Carolina Folk Drama

The tradition of "Carolina Folk Plays" began just about a century ago here at the University of North Carolina at Chapel Hill. That was when Professor Frederick Koch (1870-1944) was recruited from North Dakota to UNC by then-president Edward K. Graham. This was 1918, just as a world war was peaking and a pandemic was flaring.

Known as the founder of the Carolina Playmakers and the UNC Department of Dramatic Art, "Proff" Koch fostered a little, local revolution by turning the attention of UNC's playmaking energies onto "folk" drama. This would have national repercussions as the influence of the Carolina Playmakers spread. A man of considerable energy and creative output, he described the notion of folk drama and the Carolina process in an essay called "American Folk Drama in the Making," which serves as an introduction to the book, "American Folk Plays" (1939).

> From the first our particular interest in North Carolina has been the use of native materials and the making of fresh dramatic forms. We have found that if the young writer observes the locality with which he is most familiar and interprets it faithfully it may show him the way to the universal. If he can see the interestingness of the lives of those about him with understanding and imagination, with wonder, why may he not interpret that life in significant images for others— perhaps for all? It has been so in all lasting art.[i]

> The materials were drawn by each writer from scenes familiar and near, often from remembered adventures of his youth, from folk tales and the common tradition, and from present-day life… [ii]

Koch associated folk drama with the ways of "less sophisticated people living simple lives not seriously affected by the present-day, complex social order." [iii] Amongst the subject matters he listed were "legends, superstitions, customs, environmental differences, and the vernacular." He described the plays as mostly "realistic and human" and sometimes "imaginative and poetic." [iv] They were not necessarily tragic and indeed may well celebrate the simple joys of life.

> The chief concern of the folk dramatist is man's conflict with the forces of nature and his simple pleasure in being alive. The conflict may not be apparent on the surface in the immediate action on the

stage. But the ultimate cause of all dramatic action we classify as "folk," whether it be physical or spiritual, may be found in man's desperate struggle for existence and in his enjoyment of the world of nature. The term "folk" here then, applies to that form of drama which is earth-rooted in the life of our common humanity. [v]

Koch found folk elements in the Greeks, in Medieval drama, in Shakespeare, Goethe and Ibsen. He conceded that American playwrights of the 19th Century had used folk elements, but he offered the title of "the first significant American folk drama" to "The Great Divide" (1907) by William Vaughn Moody.[vi] Koch identifies the first use of the term "folk play" in the American theatre with Playmakers' 1919 production of "When Witches Ride" by UNC student Elizabeth Lay. She would go on to marry fellow UNC student Paul Green, who would become the premiere playwright to emerge from the Carolina Playmakers. It was Paul Green, along with Eugene O'Neill, Elmer Rice, Lynn Riggs and Maxwell Anderson, who, according to Koch, would "create an authentic folk drama of American life." [vii]

It seems that Koch helped provide a positive, nurturing environment for young playwrights. "In our way of playwriting we try to cherish the creative spark in the student." [viii] He said young playwrights must be patiently guided as they shape their materials, and those materials should be rooted in the student's own experience. He quotes a young Thomas Wolfe:

> It is a fallacy of the young writer to picture the dramatic as the unusual and remote… He is likely to choose for the setting of his first effort a New York apartment house, the Barbary Coast of San Francisco, or some remote land made dramatic by all of the perfumes of Arabia…. But the dramatic is not unusual. It is happening daily in our lives. [ix]

Another student, Dorothy Canfield, picked up from there:

> I can write nothing at all about places, people or phases of life which I do not intimately know, down to the last detail. If my life depended upon it, it does not seem to me I could possibly write a story about Siberian hunters or East-Side factory hands without having lived among them. [x]

Describing the Carolina "playmaking" process that evolved, Koch is clear that it was a kinesthetic, communal activity. First, sample Carolina plays were read by prospective playwrights individually; then, with the class, they were quickly staged, script in hand, to explore the theatrical dimensions beyond written dialogue. Students were not initially taught rules of play structure for fear they would become entangled "in the intricacies of technique." [xi] Continually reading and discussing plays and using the classroom as a staging workshop, Koch sought to "cultivat[e] in the student a feeling for good dramatic form." [xii]

When it was time to write, ideas were no sooner brought in than they were subjected to collective feedback. Indeed, what Koch described went well beyond the mores of contemporary playwriting feedback. Fellow students offered blunt critique and prescriptive solutions to perceived problems. It sounds almost like a modern TV writing room.

> So the play is not merely written, it is communally rewritten. It is really a composite product of all the members of the group, with the experience of the instructor to guide the young playwright in the complex process of building a play. We have found in our way of playwriting and theater arts that the essential thing is harmonious collaboration—a happy working together of all the members of the group. [xiii]

The vigor and productivity of this early period of the Carolina Playmakers is undeniable. Koch and company fostered not only a harmonious collective, but they brought women, African Americans, and people of different nationalities into an all-white, predominantly male campus in ways that must have been quite a challenge in the Jim Crow South. They also did not keep that work hidden away in Chapel Hill. Through publishing, through touring, they scattered that vision abroad and changed the American theatre.

Over the years, the focus on student playwriting would ebb, as Carolina Playmakers morphed into PlayMakers Repertory Company, with its status as a major L.O.R.T. regional theatre and its focus on professional production. Still, as we came up to this century milestone, a number of us here in the Department of Dramatic Art and at PlayMakers found ourselves reflecting on this visionary founder of ours and his mission to create drama that mirrored and served the lives of regular people—the "folk."

So what would a folk drama look like today? This is a question we have been investigating the past couple of years in my DRAM 331 Advanced Playwriting course. The theme of the class is "Adapting True Stories for

The Carolina Playmakers prepare their tour bus in fall 1941 before
UNC's Playmakers Theatre. "Proff" Koch is second from right.
(Photo source: PlayMakers Repertory Company)

the Stage," and we explore how to tell and structure story in a way that
suits best the subject matter, emerges organically from it, and avoids pre-
fabricated, often melodramatic, tropes. The class emphasizes two strands
of "truth-telling"—first, the history play, and second, the folk play. If the
history play seeks to tell the truth of an actual person or a factual event,
the folk play strives to share the truth of the life of a people.

For folk drama, we start by reading Proff Koch's description
summarized above. We look at "The Introduction to Playwriting"
volume (1946) by Sam Selden, Koch's successor as department chair and
director of Carolina Playmakers. We read and discuss plays that
exemplify folk drama, including plays from the volumes assembled by
Koch. Together, we develop a common understanding of how Koch's
vision might be realized in our time.

Of course, we might have some trouble, in our wired age of media,
communication and transportation, applying Koch's notion of depicting
"less sophisticated people living simple lives." At the same time, when
one digs beneath the veneer of mass-production and mass-media, there
is no lack today of local and regional "legends", "superstitions,
"customs", etc. The notion of an earth-rooted people seems to refer to

a time and a populace that has largely—though not entirely—disappeared from our lived American experience. We may still well consider how nature, struggle and pleasure might fit into a more modern prescription for folk drama.

This past semester—in the notorious spring of 2020—there were only four students in DRAM 331. That could have been the kiss of death in another class; not so with this group. They fully engaged with the course content, poured themselves into their creative work, and offered their wholehearted care in reading and responding to the work of the others. They were a worthy legacy to Proff Koch's vision and process. From these four students came four one-act plays—two history plays and four folk plays. That's right, there is certainly room for overlap between these categories.

With "A Better Life," Cole Kordus dramatizes a story that has lived in his family for generations—the coming of one of his ancestors to the United States from Poland. He sets this genuine, heartfelt piece in a 19th Century Polish village in the hour just before the rushed departure of Emilia Kuzminska. Cole took pains to make the play true to the place, character and mood of his ancestors' experience.

"The Legend of Peter Dromgoole" is the culminating creative response to a years-long investigation (and minor obsession) by writer Emily Jane MacKillop. The folklore around this would-be-martyr-to-love is a perennial source of intrigue and mystery on our campus. This draft represents Emily Jane's valiant struggle to fend off cliched forms and to find a set-up of the play that arose authentically from her perspective on the confounding and contradictory historical record.

Sorcha de Faoite is a student at National University of Ireland, Galway and was the latest in a considerable line of Irish foreign exchange students to grace my playwriting classes. It was at a quintessential UNC student event where the memories associated with the play "Kiss Fell" were triggered. She was struck with an urgency to explore her involvement in youth basketball—both the camaraderie and the isolation so keenly felt by a young, developing person. To us in the class, the dialogue sparkled with its local expression and charm.

"Ain't That Just The Way" is a refreshing, funny and topical dip into the philosophies of a group of young men in the mountains of North Carolina. Sam Bible-Sullivan explores his generation's dreams and realities, as these friends sit in nature, living out a ritual they have developed themselves, discussing the possibilities and best approaches to an uncertain future. As with "Kiss Fell," we hear a particular dialect here that is partly about place and partly about generation.

These plays are not necessarily "final drafts" after one semester of development, but I felt, even at this stage, they were worthy of amplification. Proff Koch would publish the plays of his undergraduate students and the other people who took his courses, not because their work was necessarily perfect or final, but because it was good, it was truth-telling, and, taken together, it communicated the vision of a different kind of theatre.

Mark Perry
June 2020

---

[i] Frederick Koch, *American Folk Plays*. p. xiv
[ii] Ibid, p. xv
[iii] Ibid, p. xv
[iv] Ibid, p. xv
[v] Ibid, p. xvi
[vi] Ibid, p. xviii
[vii] Ibid, p. xviii
[viii] Ibid, p. xviii
[ix] Ibid, p. xix
[x] Ibid, p. xix
[xi] Ibid, p. xxi
[xii] Ibid, p. xxii
[xiii] Ibid, p. xxvi

A Better Life

A One-Act Play by Cole Kordus

This play sprung from the idea of wanting to find "my people." I grew up pretty divorced from my larger family and in a rural area with a culture I never fully identified with; so when I was tasked to write a play about my people, my mind drew complete blank.

Life threw me a bone, though, in the form of a book called the Oman Stories, written by a relative of mine about my family's emigration to the United States over 100 years ago. Reading it, I felt an instant connection to the oldest recorded parts of the book dealing with my Great Great Grandmother Emilia Kuzminska, and her time in what is modern-day Poland. I read about how she was one of twelve children - most of whom died - and how she left her entire family behind to move to America.

What were the circumstances that made a mother send her daughter away? How did Emilia cope with leaving her entire family behind? These were the driving questions that led me through this writing process, as well as a desire to stay as close to the written truth as I possibly could. The result is A Better Life, a one act play about Emilia. I hope she would be proud, or at the very least, happy to know her story isn't forgotten.

- Cole Kordus

Summary

Emilia Kuzminska (Kizz-Min-ska) is a poor Polish girl struggling to balance taking care of her family's farm and working as a seamstress in town – but when her mother comes home with urgent news, a life-changing decision is made for her.

Characters:

EMILIA KUZMINSKA: The youngest daughter in the family, Emilia is bright, cheerful, and a bit forgetful. Since her brothers and sister moved out she has found herself increasingly stretched thin, and irritable.

JAN KUZMINSKA (PAPA): Older, wearing beat-up glasses, Jan considered himself more a philosopher and holy man than a farmer – much to the general irritation of everyone else on the farm.

MARISHA KUZMINSKA: One of the living middle children, Marisha is happily married and several weeks pregnant. She helps out Emilia from time to time at the shop in town or the family farm.

STANISLAUS ZELINSKY: Young and energetic, the red-nosed man has an unfortunate case of bad breath, and has been hopelessly in love with Emilia since they were children.

PAULINA KUZMINSKA (MAMA): Strong-willed and fierce, she has both reared her children and run the farm. Paulina had twelve children with her husband, Jan. Eight died. Her maiden name was Paulina Bukrejewska.

UNCLE ANTHONY: Jan's younger brother (by a year or two), Anthony had a thick beard and was a quiet, sad soul. He never recovered from the death of his wife.

NOTE: Uncle Anthony and Jan should be double-cast.

This play is dedicated to the many strong women of my family.

Emilia Kuzminska
(Photo source: Cole Kordus)

A Better Life

AT RISE:

(As the lights for the play come up, we see the
Kuzminska family home; a well-built but rugged
home. It has a central room that is large and open with
a fireplace and hearth, a kitchen, some wooden chairs
and a stump gathered around a table, and perhaps one
window. This is a house that has been lived in – but at
the moment is just a little too empty for the space it
holds. Small elements of decoration and memories fill
various shelves or hang from walls, and one corner is
devoted to icons, with a very worn Bible resting on a
special little shelf. There is a muddied floor by the
front door and one or two others leading to other
rooms. Jan enters the main space and kneels down in
front of the icon, praying quietly. He remains there as
Emilia enters the space. Her fingernails are stained, her
hair a bit unkempt, and face a bit sallow.)

EMILIA
Good morning, Pa-pa.

JAN
Morning, child. Sleep well?

EMILIA
But of course, *[She kisses him on the cheek – it wasn't true]* I know you're
loathe to face the morning dew – but perhaps in the afternoon you
could help till the south field?

JAN

Ach, you know I would, but my leg is acting up once again. God willing, soon I'll be able to help.

EMILIA

Whatever you say Papa. *[Beat]* Do you think Cousin Nina will come soon?

JAN

Undoubtedly so! I've been praying to the Lord and he has given me strong indications; she shall arrive soon enough.

EMILIA

I pray you're right, I'm not sure we could make it through another winter without her help. We're already getting low on grains and preserves… Oh, I hope the border crossing goes well…

JAN

[Stands and moves to Emilia] The faithful are always tested Emilia, that is the way of things. But He will always give us the strength to persevere through all suffering. Even so, I have faith that Aunt Nina will arrive in good health, don't you worry.

EMILIA

I hope so.

JAN

Know so. *[Beat]* Have you considered Stanislaus's proposal?

EMILIA

Ach, Papa! *[begins putting on one boot, hands shaking a bit]* You and Mama are absolutely horrible with this – for the last time no, I have no interest in Stanislaus.

JAN

Very well, very well. Your mother asked that I –

EMILIA

Honestly, Papa, *[standing, with only one boot on]* what makes her think that Stanislaus is a good match for me?

JAN

They have land to their name – and the boy is a good, devout Christian fellow. You could do much worse.

EMILIA

I could do much better! His breath is just atrocious – and he's shorter than me – so you know it must be bad for me to notice.

JAN

Mhmm. *[Has lost interest in the conversation]*

EMILIA

Besides, I haven't the time. The shop has… has been taking up all my days recently.

JAN

Mhm.

EMILIA

I have to open up early today – so you'll have to get the geese from the pond and bring them closer, yes?

JAN

Mhm.

EMILIA

[She sees he isn't listening] And make sure you cut down all the trees around the house.

JAN

Mhm.

EMILIA

And you're okay if I move to Moscow and marry the Tzar, yes?

JAN

Yes, yes. *[Emilia strides over and claps her hands together by his ear – and he jumps in surprise.]* Ach! What, what is it?

EMILIA

The geese! They need to be brought up from the pond.

JAN

I thought you would do that?

EMILIA

I. Cannot. I have an order that needs to be done *today*.

JAN

[grunts] More silly dresses?

EMILIA

Those 'silly dresses' paid for that new coat of yours, now, didn't they?

JAN

Apologies, dear. You know how I feel about that shop.

EMILIA

I do. *[She looks at him expectantly]*

JAN

And…?

EMILIA

Geese! Papa! The Geese!

JAN

Don't raise your voice to me – yes, I will fetch the geese. I thought we had settled the matter.

EMILIA

My god, sometimes –

JAN

What was that? *[Warning tone]*

EMILIA

Sorry, Papa.

                              JAN
Good girl. All's forgiven.

                    (Emilia turns and lets out a tight, clenched breath of
                    anger before letting go. Marisha – Emilia's older sister
                    – enters.)

                              MARISHA
Good morning Papa,\ good morning – Emilia?

                              JAN
\Morning!

                              EMILIA
Morning, Marisha.

                              MARISHA
[Crossing to her] Sleep poorly again?

                              EMILIA
Yes.

                              MARISHA
Come, come, I'll fetch a cup of milk.

                              EMILIA
No, no, really, I must get going.

                              MARISHA
To the shop? An order? *[Emilia nods, beginning to gather her things]* I would
offer to help, but…

                              EMILIA
But what? *[Barely listening]*

                              MARISHA
I'll… say it later.

                              EMILIA
Perfect! Well… I'm off. Will you be around this evening?

MARISHA

I'm not sure, most likely not.

EMILIA

Then I shall see you soon. Bye Papa. Bye, Marisha.

(Emilia is about to walk out the front door when she realizes she only has one boot on. She sets all of her things back down and is halfway through pulling it on when the front door swings open, and none other than the aforementioned Stanislaus enters.)

STANISLAUS

Hello? Ah! Mr. Kuzminska I – *[sees Emilia]* – Oh! Greetings Emilia!

EMILIA

Greetings, Stanislaus…

MARISHA

Hello, Stan.

(Jan has stood, Marisha moves closer to Emilia, and Stanislaus is staring at Emilia dreamily – for she is the prettiest woman in all Poland to him.)

JAN

Stanislaus? Ahem! What – *[Notices Emilia]* I thought you'd left?

EMILIA

I forgot my boot. *[She has finished putting it on]*

JAN

But you're wearing it, my dear. *[Back to Stanislaus]* What is it, my child?

STANISLAUS

Hmm? Oh! Yes! Greetings Mr. Kuzminska!

JAN

Greetings, Stanislaus. What has you in such a rush?

STANISLAUS

I'm terribly sorry – it's my brother – he's fallen ill again and we were hoping – well that you could come and watch over him, as you do.

JAN

I would be delighted to do so – I can beseech God on his behalf. He's ill? *[Stanislaus nods]* Hm… I can think of some passages to read for better health…

EMILIA

Stan, what exactly, is wrong with your brother?

STANISLAUS

[Moving Closer to her] Oh, he's very ill, he is! Forehead's hot, skin pale, hard to leave bed and-

EMILIA

[Putting some distance between his breath] Perhaps a good hot soak or some tea would help? I know Papa has work here at the farm to do.

JAN

Emilia, darling, the boy needs prayer – Increasingly, I feel that this is my purpose here in the world; to bring comfort and the wisdom of God to those who need it. Was it not just last week that the Burkawa's travelled two whole days just to speak with me?

EMILIA

Papa –

STANISLAUS

Please, Miss Emilia? My folks would feel a lot better if he could offer some words of kindness… He's got the runs! And last time your father came, it cleared right up in a day's time – people are saying he's a true holyman!

JAN

[Thoroughly Pleased] You flatter me Stanislaus, you do, but there's no need to say more, child, I'm sure Emilia understands. *[He takes his Bible and gives her a look]* A man's life is on the line. *[to Stanislaus]* Have you horses?

STANISLAUS

No – I was walking on the main road here.

JAN

Ah, a brisk walk then. Well… it should do me good!

EMILIA

Papa, what about your leg?

JAN

Hm? Oh! Well, it feels much better now, and besides, one must always be ready to do God's work.

EMILIA

Papa – !

STANISLAUS

Please Emilia? I would be ever so grateful.

EMILIA

Ach, fine. \ No one listens to me anyway.

JAN

\ Excellent – it's settled. Come, Stanislaus, let's not keep your brother waiting. *[He exits and Emilia buries her head in her hands. Jan pokes his head back in]* Oh! And Emilia?

EMILIA

What! Papa, what?

JAN

The geese! Someone must take care of them. God be with you! *[He exits]*

(Emilia lets out a pained noise of frustration and Marisha gives her a cup of milk.)

MARISHA

Drink up, it'll soothe your nerves.

(The door opens again and Jan makes an apologetic gesture before grabbing his coat and waving goodbye once more. Emilia gives Marisha a pointed look before speaking.)

EMILIA

Our Papa is the most obnoxious man in all of Poland! The moment there's work to be done around here he vanishes! And what gets done?

MARISHA

Nothing\

EMILIA

Nothing! Nothing gets done – and Mama is always upset and has to work extra hard to make up for it and I wind up having to leave work early so that I can be of some use as well – not to mention that Mama *and* Uncle Anthony are off with the horses, so I shall have to walk – and-!

MARISHA

Oh, I know, I know! It's all one big mess – come, come. *[She gives her a hug]* I hope Uncle Anthony comes back soon – he can always sort you out whenever you get all wound up.

EMILIA

[Swatting her] Very funny! Ach, I swear, if I left this place would fall apart.

MARISHA

[Somewhat tensely] Oh, don't say such things, you know it isn't true. *[Beat]* I take it you're still unenthused with Stanislaus?

EMILIA

No, no, no – I have already had this conversation with Papa – though I swear it was Mama's words.

MARISHA

My, my! You seem to be swearing a lot more now that you work in town. But – point taken, I shan't speak of Stanislaus any further. *[beat]* Have you... thought about the boat?

EMILIA

Boat? What – *[Beat]* No. No. I haven't, and I won't.

MARISHA

Emilia… you know that I would miss you terribly – I would be
heartbroken – but you should at the very least think about it; it makes
sense.

EMILIA

What sense is there in abandoning my family?!

MARISHA

You wouldn't be abandoning us –

EMILIA

I would! I'd be leaving you all behind, the farm would fall into disarray,
I wouldn't be able to see you, or Mama, or our brothers, and the shop
– OH! The Shop!

MARISHA

What about it?

EMILIA

I have to get there soon!

MARISHA

Why? An order?

EMILIA

Yes! Miss Nowicki asked for her dress today – and I have yet to
properly hem the whole shirt, and the wooden shanks are no good, I
shall have to find new ones…

MARISHA

I'll take care of the geese, don't worry.

EMILIA

Would you?

MARISHA

Of course, of course. I'll do it before I leave for home.

EMILIA

You'll remember to try and speak like Mama and I? They like our voices best…

MARISHA

[Imitating Emilia] Ach, fine.

EMILIA

Marisha! I love you! Oh, I wish you were around more often. Ach! And I didn't even ask – why are you leaving this evening? I thought you were going to wait here for Mama, Aunt Nina, and Uncle Anthony. They aren't supposed to be home until late tonight or tomorrow.

MARISHA

I know… I know, but… I think I need to tell my husband something.

EMILIA

What is it?

MARISHA

You must promise not to tell Mama – not yet.

EMILIA

Did Cyprian do something? Is it bad news?

MARISHA

It's not bad news, not at all… in fact, it's very good news… *[Slow, creeping smile]*

EMILIA

No!

MARISHA

Yes!

(Emilia lets out a happy shriek and rushes over, embracing her. The two laugh and dance for a moment before settling down)

EMILIA

When! How long have you known?

MARISHA

It's recent, very recent – but today, I had another bout of morning sickness – that's the third time this week! Oh, but you mustn't tell Mama.

EMILIA

Why?

MARISHA

Well… this… isn't the first time.

EMILIA

Oh, oh. *[This is a familiar sadness to the Family]* I understand, of course, but when would a good time be?

MARISHA

Further along, further along. Don't fret – I will of course tell Mama before I start to show.

EMILIA

Good, good. Do you need money? Orders from the shop have been coming in and I have some money to spare.

MARISHA

Oh please, don't worry about us – worry about yourself! You look absolutely awful – and your shaking. Are you sure you have to go into that dreadful place?

EMILIA

… I must work. If I don't, what'll happen when the food stores run out and we can't afford food?

MARISHA

But there's no need to work yourself so hard! You said it yourself, Aunt Nina should be coming and she always brings…

EMILIA

Brings…?

MARISHA

Do you hear that?

EMILIA

Hear- *[the two pause as the sounds of horses and a small carriage can be heard just outside]* Horses? Could it be Mama?

MARISHA

I thought that she wasn't due back till tomorrow?

EMILIA

She isn't… *[Moving towards the Door]* Perhaps –

> (The door opens and Paulina and Uncle Anthony come in. Anthony is grim – but he normally appears so. More worryingly, Paulina appears a little shaken; but holds herself together with the composure of a woman who has endured much and will endure more still)

EMILIA

Mama! Uncle Anthony! You're back early.

ANTHONY

Aye. We rushed home.

MARISHA

Mama, I… *[Was going to greet her but sees the mood]* Mama what happened?

PAULINA

Anthony would you mind taking care of the horses?

ANTHONY

Aye, I can do that. *[He exits]*

MARISHA

Mama?

EMILIA

What's going on?

PAULINA

Marisha, sit. *[She does so and Paulina puts a hand to her face for a moment, before:]* Cousin Nina is dead.

(Marisha gasps and slumps – it's good she sat down – and Emilia is shocked)

EMILIA

My God, how! What happened?

PAULINA

She was crossing the border – like usual. But apparently the guard she normally bribes was gone on leave and when they commanded her to stop… she didn't.

EMILIA

That's horrible!

PAULINA

Smuggling has always been a risky business… Naturally everything she had was confiscated by the border guard. And I don't even know if her family knows…

MARISHA

[Beat] She was pregnant, wasn't she?

(Paulina simply nods and it is now that the tragedy of the situation really hits Emilia.)

PAULINA

… I won't postpone it any longer.

EMILIA

Postpone what?

MARISHA

… Wait Mama, you're not talking about –

PAULINA

I am. Go and fetch a bag from upstairs – the nice one, if you can. Pack it with some clothes and food. *[Marisha nods and runs off]*

EMILIA

Wait… Mama no.

PAULINA

Yes. You know I've be talking with your Aunt Frances – she still has a job and a home for you in America, and… well. You're leaving. You're going to live with her in America.

EMILIA

Mama!

PAULINA

It's already settled – Your father agrees with me that it's best, and Aunt Frances just sent us the money needed to buy a ticket.

EMILIA

When! How? Last we spoke, this was just a wild idea that you proposed! I can't leave now!

PAULINA

You can, and you will! What do I always tell you, Emilia?

EMILIA

[Mumbling]

PAULINA

Speak up!

EMILIA

'Pray as I do every day, that you do not die and leave your children Orphans.'

PAULINA

Precisely so. I will not leave you without prospects and a home, as I once was. A mother ought to give a better life to her children – which is what I aim to do. *[Beat]* Emilia, darling… there simply isn't enough here for you. In America… there is opportunity.

EMILIA

But this… this is my home? *[Teary]* I can't just… leave you all…

PAULINA

You must. You will. *[Beat]* Ach. Where is your sister?

> (Paulina leaves to find Marisha, leaving Emilia alone for a moment. She brings a hand to her mouth and paces, mind whirling. Anthony opens the doors and returns from having put the horses away)

EMILIA

Uncle! What's all this talk of me leaving so suddenly? Do you know what this is all about?

ANTHONY

Aye. I do.

EMILIA

… Well!?

ANTHONY

Your mother thinks it best.

EMILIA

She doesn't get to just send me off –

ANTHONY

I happen to agree with her.

EMILIA

[Taken aback] What?

ANTHONY

[Sitting down on the stump] Do you remember tending the Geese when you were young?

EMILIA

Of course. I remember following them out to the pond and forest. Sleeping with them under the stars with Marisha and Stanislaus and Kolya. Why?

ANTHONY

Do you also remember coming home cold, tired, and hungry?

EMILIA

… I do.

ANTHONY

This home… it is our home. This farm, it is our life. But it is a hard life, Emilia. And a sad home.

EMILIA

No, Uncle, I don't –

ANTHONY

Please, Emilia. You know I'm right. Look – out the window, there, what do you see? *[Beat]* I see my buried nieces and nephews. And were I to move to the left, I could see the well where… where Kiki fell. *[Beat]* This home is a hard home to be in. I know you feel it. A part of me believes it's for this very reason you spend so much time in that shop of yours.

EMILIA

We have much work…

ANTHONY

And you're up all night and all morning doing it. You come home exhausted and red-eyed from all the concoctions and dyes you have in there.

EMILIA

…

ANTHONY

Face it, Emilia… there's not much for you here.

(Marisha and Paulina enter. Marisha sees how Emilia is faring and goes to comfort her while Paulina begins to gather some food)

EMILIA

I just… how could you say that, when I have you? Mama? Marisha? *[She hugs her sister]* I can't leave you…

MARISHA

Emilia. I'm going to miss you, so very much!

EMILIA

Ach! Don't say that! You act as if it has already been decided!

MARISHA

Hasn't it?

EMILIA

I… *[She looks around]* I'm starting to feel as if I don't have much choice in the matter…

MARISHA

It's for the best. It makes my heart heavy, but I think it is for the best.

EMILIA

How could you say that, Marisha? Especially now that –

MARISHA

Emilia. Emilia, why do you think I've brought up the idea so much?
How many times have I spoken to you about the boat, or travel in
general? I've been trying to convince you for weeks.

EMILIA

Yes, but I thought I would have more time, I thought that I would be
able to get things in order here…

MARISHA

If you got all the time you wanted, you would never leave. All you
would do is try to fight it – the very thing you're doing right now! All
you want is time to come up with a good reason to stay.

EMILIA

And why shouldn't I?? You are my *family!* I can't just leave you all…

PAULINA

Haven't you already? Spending all day, all night at that dress shop of
yours?

EMILIA

That is nowhere near the same as being in another country!

MARISHA

Really, though, Emilia… listen to me. I love you so very much – and if
you go, I will miss you every day, of course I will. But I have my
Cyprian and… well, you know. Both our brothers have wives and – by
God, I can't remember the last time I saw either of them. Mama and
Papa will be fine.

EMILIA

Mama does all the work on the farm – what if –

PAULINA

I have Anthony to help out around the farm.

ANTHONY

Aye, she does.

PAULINA

Really now, Emilia, you're simply being dramatic. *[She sets the fully packed bag down near the door]* We will be fine.

EMILIA

It… it's all just… so sudden! Surely, you're not suggesting I leave now?

PAULINA

I am.

EMILIA

But… I haven't gotten to say goodbye to Papa – or Roman, or Aloysius!

PAULINA

You know what he would say? He would say that this is part of His intent, and that your great trial is to accept it. Your father and I have spoken about this for a long time. We both agree. *[Beat]* And your brothers will support your decision – you can always write them.

EMILIA

Ah! But that's precisely the problem; this isn't my decision, it's yours! You've already decided what's to become of me.

PAULINA

You do have a choice.

EMILIA

I…

ANTHONY

Emilia… Cousin Nina was… a reminder to us. We want to get you out before things get worse.

EMILIA

Before what gets worse?

ANTHONY

The Russians lost their *entire* navy in the Pacific! How much longer do you think our *generous* occupiers are going to be able to control us? Or prevent others from seeking our lands?

MARISHA

Please, Uncle. I really don't think that the Russians would abandon us.

ANTHONY

We were just in Agustow and unrest is all that's being spoken of; talk of the Russians losing their grip on us.

PAULINA

We must stop this talk; it's bad luck. *[Beat, to Emilia]* But yes. Emilia, this is part of the reason why it must be soon. The border between us and Germany is getting tighter and tighter every passing week. We might not be able to get out at all, in a month or two from now.

EMILIA

Well if things are so bad here, why don't we all leave together?

PAULINA

Out of the question.

ANTHONY

And our pocketbook.

MARISHA

Emilia, sister. *[She holds her]* We all have a future here. You can still… do anything. Be anything. Find someone you actually love and wouldn't marry just to appease Mama or Papa.

EMILIA

If I left and something happened… I could never forgive myself.

PAULINA

Nothing will happen. And if it does, you have nothing to forgive yourself for. I, on the other hand… will not lose another daughter. I won't.

(There is a tense moment of silence)

EMILIA
Where would I even go, once I'm over there?

PAULINA
It will be a two-week trip to America, and from then you'll take a coach to a place called… Mill-wau-kee. It's in the north, I think. Aunt Frances will meet you there.

EMILIA
… Must I really, truly go?

PAULINA
Yes. You must.

> (Emilia stands and moves towards the kitchen and stump, looking out the window, before turning back to the fireplace and putting a hand to her heart)

EMILIA
I… truly believed that I would see this place for the rest of my time.

MARISHA
Hey… it is only a house. Only a home.

ANTHONY
And an old, sad home at that.

PAULINA
Emilia… *[She moves to her and takes her hands]* You will make a new house. You will make a better home. You will find a loving, kind husband with much better prospects than anyone you could hope to find here… And we will write you letters, and you will write us letters, and you will have a lovely, large family. You will be so, so very happy and your children will love you dearly and… and they won't **ever** have to worry about being orphaned.

EMILIA

I love you, Ma, *[Emilia hugs Paulina before turning to Marisha]* Will… will
you be okay?

MARISHA

Truly. I will. Cyprian takes good care of me. And I can always work at
the shop, if need be.

EMILIA

[Sniffing] I suppose… I suppose Miss Nowicki won't be getting her
dress today, will she?

MARISHA

Probably not,

EMILIA

Uncle –

ANTHONY

No need to say good-bye yet, I'm taking you to the boat.

EMILIA

Good… Mama, you will be staying here then?

PAULINA

Someone must look after the house… and I see your father's gone
again. So.

EMILIA

The… the geese are down by the south pond. The water for today's
already been drawn. I… I suppose the horses won't be needing tending,
since we… we'll be taking them… *[To Marisha]* Here… the key to the
shop. I… won't be needing it anymore. You can trust Helena to run
things when I'm – when you're not… around.

MARISHA

Of course.

(There's a pause)

PAULINA

[Gently, firmly] There's no use in delaying. It's time.

(Emilia nods, hugs Marisha again, then Paulina)

EMILIA

I'm going to miss you both… so, so much…

MARISHA

As will I!

PAULINA

You will be better off, I promise.

(The three have a moment)

EMILIA

Well… well then. *[She shoulders her pack]* It's time, isn't it. *[She turns to Anthony]* … Shall… shall we leave, then?

ANTHONY

Aye.

(The two head for the door. Emilia trips on the door still and turns. She looks at her mother, her sister, the house, then lets go. She leaves. Paulina and Marisha move to the window and wait and watch, then begin waving, before slowly stopping. Marisha is still sniffling. Paulina moves away and sits down heavily – then begins to cry)

MARISHA

Oh, oh Mama, - ! *[She rushes over and embraces her mother]*

PAULINA

I… I won't ever see her again… My darling girl…

MARISHA

We might, Mama, we might…

PAULINA

Have I… orphaned my own daughter by doing this?

MARISHA

No, mama, no… shh…. It will be alright… she'll be okay…

> (Lights fade down, leaving the two huddled together
> and barely illuminated. An empty space is lit and
> Emilia steps into it)

EMILIA

I remember looking back at the farm as we left… staring at the house, the well, the hill with my buried brothers and sisters… and I remember feeling sad. Sad because it was the last time I would see my Mama. Sad because I left Marisha behind. But the further and further we got away… the more the pain faded to a dull ache.

[Beat]

Uncle Anthony would talk to me every once in a while, but mostly we were quiet. There wasn't much to say, really. Crossing the border was tense, and it took a while, but we were let through and made our way to a German town along a river – I never learned the names, my German is bad. Leaving Uncle Anthony behind was almost… easy. Compared to everything else.

[Beat]

The boat is crowded. I've met three other Polish girls here, and they seem quite nice. I think we're going to stick together. The Germans are being rude and nasty to us… but I'm used to that. I write to help calm myself… and remember. I don't want to forget anything about that last day. I still can't believe I never got to say goodbye to my father… I hope they'll all be okay without me…

[Beat]

America… what's it really like? I've heard stories – that it's a place for everyone, that you can make a living there, that you can be happy… can it all be true? I don't speak any English… I hope that won't be too big a problem…

[Beat]

The new world draws near; I don't know what's going to happen to me but I do… I do hope. I hope I never have to send any child of mine away. I pray I never leave my children orphans.

The Legend of Peter Dromgoole

A Chapel Hill Urban Legend

A One-Act Play by Emily Jane MacKillop

The Legend of Peter Dromgoole is based on the university student, Peter Dromgoole, who went missing in the spring of 1833. Over time, Peter's disappearance has become a legend which has escalated from a simple disappearance to an epic duel over the love of a Miss. Fannie. The duel itself has multiple endings but all have the common theme of death and heartbreak, with the more recent addition of the ghost of Peter and Fannie and a connection to the elusive secret society, The Knights of the Order of Gimghoul. The Carolina Folk play is all about writing what you know, and writing the story of the people. This play speaks of a legend that has lingered on the edge of UNC student culture for nearly 200 years, evolving with the students that tell the story, and highlighting the ever present conflict between truth and rumor. The Legend of Peter Dromgoole plants the seeds that have become the present day rumors of what exactly happened to Peter Dromgoole, did he run away? join the army? Or did he actually die in a duel?

- Emily Jane MacKillop

Cast of Characters

Peter Dromgoole;   18, a student at the university, gets into trouble frequently. A ghost

Fannie;   17, naive, loves Peter and best friends with William.

William Kittrell;   18, loves Fannie and Peter. Also A ghost

Nancy;   The owner of a college bar, wise and reassuring.

Richard;   Nancy's son; wants to sit at the adult table.

James Williams;   Peter's roommate and friends with William. First generation college student, has something to prove.

George C. Dromgoole;   Peter's uncle and an alcoholic

Setting

Nancy's Bar. There are three doors, One to the kitchen, one to the outside on the opposite side of the bar, and the main entrance. Perhaps there is an upstairs

Time

April 24th, 1833

Author's note

… is a pause of anxiety or being unsure of one's train of thought
--- is a pause where the words are unable to be spoken
/ is when one character interrupts another and the dialogue should overlap

Peter and William are only seen by one character at a time

The Old Well and Old East Dorm on the UNC Campus. Old East
is where Peter Dromgoole is said to have lived while on campus.
(Photo source: Emily Jane MacKillop)

The Legend of Peter Dromgoole
A Chapel Hill Urban Legend

SCENE 1

(Lights up on PETER DROMGOOLE and
WILLIAM KITTRELL. They stand back to back in
an isolated pool of light. It is raining. They walk three
paces away from each other in sync. A beat after the
third step they quickly turn around and shoot, almost
immediately PETER falls to the ground. A scream
from offstage. Blackout)

SCENE 2

(Lights up on Nancy's bar. There is nothing special
about it. PETER, who fell asleep writing at the bar,
wakes suddenly with a start when something offstage
breaks)

NANCY

Damn it Richard! I swear to God if you break even one more glass it
will be the last thing you do
            (NANCY enters with a bucket of water and a rag)
Ah well good morning Peter, have a nice nap did we?

            (PETER slowly wakes up during this exchange, he
            puts his writing into two envelopes that are already
            stamped and addressed. NANCY is cleaning and
            straightening up the bar and absentmindedly takes the
            letters and puts them behind the bar by the cashbox)

PETER

Is it really morning? Did you let me sleep here all night?

NANCY

Yes it's morning, and let you sleep here, I couldn't wake ya, you slept like the dead

PETER

I'm sorry Nancy, I really did not mean to fall asleep here...again

NANCY

I swear you must sleep here more than you sleep at home, I should start charging you rent

PETER

And I'd pay it, if I'd get a proper bed. It's easier to get work done here

NANCY

Get work done? Well that'd be a first

PETER

I do work...sometimes...when it's interesting

NANCY

Mhm

PETER

It's not my fault all the classes are useless

NANCY

I reckon there are several young men that'd much ruther be in your position that would find those classes very interesting

PETER

And everyone is so serious all the time, I don't get how they can sit in an office all day reading books and holding intellectual conversations/

NANCY

Did ya get another letter from your father?

PETER

Professor Mitchell wrote him expressing his...displeasure with my time
on campus

NANCY

It seems that he did not respond too kindly to that

PETER

I cannot do anything right, I am so sick of this place. I am going to just
leave and do something else somewhere else

NANCY

And what are you gonna be doing? And where do you think you'll be
doin it?

PETER

I could go traveling. Maybe try my hand out west with the gold mines
or go stay with my relatives in Ireland.

NANCY

And how would you get there? With what money would you be doing
this traveling with?

PETER

Well, then I'll get a job along the way, or stow away inside a train or
boat.

NANCY

And what of Miss. Fannie? She'll be all tore up if you just up and leave
her like this

PETER

Oh get off it, I can dream

NANCY

Well it's time to wake up- this is your life. You go to a good university,
you have a beautiful lady dying for your affection and a father, although
strong willed, wants the best for you-

PETER

I know, I know. I've heard this speech a thousand times.

NANCY

Oh honey, I know it's tough, but you've got your whole life ahead of you- but first you gotta get your degree and make some money of your own. Now up and at 'em you're gonna help me clean this place up as payment for your bed here

PETER

I really didn't mean to fall asleep here-

NANCY

I know but it looks like it's gunna start pouring any minute, so there's no sense in ya leaving right now and there'll be breakfast for ya when you are done. You can get started with the floors.

(something breaks offstage)

RICHARD
(Offstage)

Nothing Broke! I swear

(More things breaking)

NANCY
(Nancy sighs)

Provided Richard doesn't break everything in my kitchen

(NANCY hurries offstage, PETER stands and takes the bucket and rag and exits to the outside through the side door. There is a clap of thunder that seems to come from far off in the distance, it might be raining but JAMES enters from the main door out of breath but dry. PETER re-enters when he hears JAMES, but JAMES does not see nor hear PETER and seems to be talking to himself. This is a rehearsed speech)

JAMES

Peter! I've been looking for you all morning/ you're Uncle George is in town and is looking for you/. He showed up at our room early this morning, and I realized that I haven't seen you for a couple of days. /Apparently there's some rumors going around about you running off and your uncle seems to believe them to be true. I've been studying for exams so I've hardly left the library. I don't really care that you been laying out all /night, I've heard all your excuses- but we've got exams coming up and/ I like to be prepared for them. Which means I need to be able to study and focus/ and not be stressing about you. And I know your family can be pushy and imposing, but I figure I don't have the same luxuries you do. I actually care/ 'bout my education and I don't want to tell you what to do. You ain't care as much as I do, and that's fine- 'til it affects me. I just need you to find him/ and leave me out of it.

PETER

/Really?? My uncle?
/Why?

/I'm sorry I was here writing until late last night and seem to have fallen asleep

/I will go find him later

/I am sorry about this-

/you know how my family can be

/I care-

/I will deal with him

(PETER exits through the side door in a huff at the same time as another clap of thunder. NANCY and RICHARD enter simultaneously)

NANCY

Ah, James I haven't seen you 'round here in ages, what brings ya here this morning

JAMES

Just lookin' for Peter

NANCY

Ah well I hope you find him, would you like to stay for breakfast? It ain't rainin so Richard' fixin' to go out and get the eggs. If you'd like to wait a bit you are more than welcome to have some

JAMES

No thank you ma'am, I just needed to find Peter. If you do see him, do let him know that his uncle is looking for him.

RICHARD

I heard Peter disappeared

NANCY

Richard, don't be silly where'd ya hear a thing like that?

RICHARD

Daddy was talkin' about it with Edward, said he heard Peter and someone yelling outside- said it seemed serious. I hear tell they got into a fight

NANCY

Edward is a no 'count drunk and you're fathers no better. Now here, skedaddle- get me a dozen eggs and drop that mail behind the bar to be posted

(RICHARD takes a few coins from NANCY, goes behind the bar to grab the mail and the basket. As he runs outside, NANCY yell's after him)

It's gonna rain so be quick and for the love of God don't break any of 'em eggs!

(to JAMES)

I'll be lucky if he comes back with three unbroken eggs. Now, what was this about Peter?

JAMES

His uncle is in town lookin fer him

NANCY

What for?

JAMES

Dunno, I figure it's due to all the mischief he been causin 'round campus

NANCY

Ah that does tend to rile his family up, well if I see Peter I'll be sure to let him know his uncle is in town. Now you sure you don't wanna stay fer breakfast? I reckon we might have plenty of eggs

JAMES

No I'm quite alright ma'am I gotta get on goin to the library to study

NANCY

Ah yes, it's about that time of year again. How ya feelin bout your exams?

JAMES

I ain't too worried, but I'll feel a whole lot better after some more studyin'

NANCY

Of course, well I won't keep you then. Oh! And if you see Peter before I do, tell him he left some letters here, looks like they're ready to be posted but I wanna make sure he knew they went

JAMES

I might could do that for ya ma'am. Have a good day

NANCY

You too

(JAMES exits and FANNIE enters, they do not see each other)

FANNIE

Good morning Mrs. Nancy

NANCY

Why Good morning to you too Miss. Fannie, what brings you 'round here?

FANNIE

Well, I was just wonderin if you'd seen Peter recently

NANCY

Well my, my, that boy is the talk of the town today. It seems everybody be lookin for him

FANNIE

So you haven't seen him?

NANCY

I'm sorry sweetheart, been here all morning, you know what though- it is exam season maybe he's holed up somewhere studyin

FANNIE

When has he ever studied for anything?

NANCY

I know Peter thinks he's smarter than everyone here, but I reckon he's tryin to turn over a new leaf. Especially given that you're father's one a' his professors, and I figure he won't look to kindly on your relationship with Peter if he does poorly in his class

FANNIE

I guess, but Peter's never disappeared like this before

NANCY

Oh darlin he disappears all the time, he just ain't disappeared on you before. Give him a few days and don't get all tore up bout it, he'll likely see you as soon as the exams are over.
                    (A clap of thunder)
Oh my, looks like it's gonna start rainin' any minute, I'm gotta go get my things off the line- but Miss. Fannie, Please don't fret and stay for breakfast, I'll be fixin some eggs

FANNIE

I'd love to...but didn't I see Richard running outside right before I came in? We're likely not gunna have enough eggs.

NANCY

Oh one can hope. Well I'll be right back..

(NANCY exits as WILLIAM enters with another clap
of thunder)

WILLIAM

Mornin Miss. Fannie. It looks like its about to start stormin real bad, I
saw you come in here and I thought I'd stop in to say hey and avoid the
rain

FANNIE

William, you know you can call me Fannie, we've been friends for ages

(Goes to hugs WILLIAM, but he steps away
deflecting)

WILLIAM

Oh I know, but you're of age now, it seems right that I start calling you
Miss

FANNIE

You know that I ain't no different than I was before and you callin me
'Miss. Fannie' just seems silly. It's Fannie. Plan and simple.

WILLIAM

Alright alright, just Fannie it is

FANNIE

How are you? I haven't seen you in ages

WILLIAM

Oh that ain't true. How are you?

FANNIE

I'm… I'm… I don't know I'm worried about Peter

WILLIAM

Peter? Why?

FANNIE

I haven't seen him in ages either, have you spoken with him?

WILLIAM

No, not since our quarrel, I said some pretty harsh things- Him as well but I haven't seen him since

FANNIE

That's so unlike him, I mean, it's not not like him to quarrel, you two get into spats all the time but he's never completely disappeared due to it

WILLIAM

Well did you talk to Mrs. Nancy about it? She's probably the only adult figure he respects around here and she knows him quite well

FANNIE

Yes...She said he's probably studying for the exams

WILLIAM

Peter? Study?

FANNIE

Exactly!

WILLIAM

I am sure it is nothing

FANNIE

But where is he?

WILLIAM

Who knows, but he will show up eventually, always does

FANNIE

Are you sure?

WILLIAM

I am positive, You know how Peter can be

FANNIE

That's what Mrs. Nancy said too…

WILLIAM

See, if something was happenin with Peter she would be the first to know

FANNIE

I'm sure you are right. Okay- Tell me something to get my mind off of this, how are you really? I hardly see you/ anymore

WILLIAM

Oh that's not/ true

FANNIE

And when I do see ya, your with James or arguing with Peter

WILLIAM

That's not true… Peter and I don't just argue/

FANNIE

But we don't talk anymore

WILLIAM

Well.. I reckon you're right… and I'm sorry. I've had a lot on my mind recently

FANNIE

Well talk to me, maybe I can help. Is it 'bout university?

WILLIAM

No, college is fine

FANNIE

Is it your family? Are they pressuring you again? I swear I thought it was only daughters they insisted get married right away

WILLIAM

No well yes, they are the same as ever. There was actually someone I might been interested in, but it's… well it's complicated

FANNIE

Really? Who? You must tell me

WILLIAM

I don't want to get your hopes up to soon, I'm sure they are not interested in me

FANNIE

Well of course they would! Who wouldn't be!

WILLIAM

Well you weren't for one

FANNIE

That's because you are practically my brother, if we hadn't grown up together you might have had a chance

WILLIAM

I know, I know. And you're in love with Peter,
                    (to himself)
although if there was anyone I coulda chosen to fall in love with it would be you

FANNIE

William stop you're making me blush. Now tell me about this girl that has caught your eye- Is she pretty? Smart? Is she nice?

WILLIAM

Well, um yes to all three

FANNIE

And?

WILLIAM

And?

FANNIE

And who is it?! Come on- Give me a hint? Is it someone I know?

WILLIAM

...Yes... it is someone you would know

FANNIE

Professor Mitchell's daughter?

WILLIAM

Who? Oh no of course not, she is very... loud

FANNIE

Loud? What does that mean

WILLIAM

Loud? Well loud means you know... Just loud

FANNIE

Hmmm... Annabelle?

WILLIAM

Annabelle?

FANNIE

Nevermind- Who is it? Tell me please?

WILLIAM

It's no one- don't worry about it

FANNIE
(excitedly)

But we could go on double dates! Have a picnic out at Piney Prospect
by our rock, Father would be much more willing to let me spend time
with Peter if he knew you'd be there

WILLIAM

I don't know about that. Peter wouldn't want me to intrude on your
time together and the rock is a special place for us- for you guys- for
Peter that I don't know if that would be right and-

(RICHARD enters, wet and covered in dirt, quite loudly and magnificently falls over with the eggs, but the eggs appear to be safe)

FANNIE

Oh Peter would think it's a lovely idea!

RICHARD
(getting to his feet excitedly)
Are you talking about Peter!? I heard he died!

(NANCY, having heard the commotion, enters)

NANCY

Richard! Hold your tongue. Where in tarnation would you hear a thing like that and why would you choose to repeat it!?

RICHARD

Tommy told me while I was waiting fer the eggs, he said he heard it from Susan who heard it from her older brother who overheard two boys talkin about it in the lavatory. And James said that Peter's uncle is 'ere looking for him! So it gotta be true

NANCY

Disappeared and dead are two very different things- Now I ain't wanna hear another thing about Peter from you unless you know it is absolutely true ya hear?

RICHARD

Yes mama

NANCY

Good. Now gimme those eggs- I asked for a dozen why are there only eight in here? Well I see that yer a mess- go get yourself cleaned up breakfast will be ready shortly.
(RICHARD exits stumbling a few times. NANCY notices FANNIE, who looks distraught)
Well I reckon' it musta started pouring outside. Fannie dear? Will ya come help me in the kitchen?

FANNIE

What? Oh um yes of course.

NANCY

Come on dear
            (while they exit)
I reckon everything is just fine, it all just hearsay. 'member that time
everyone got all riled up when someone said Reverend Riley fell asleep
in his barn and his dog got loose, knocked over a lantern and burned
the whole place down with him inside? Well it turned out to be just a
brush fire caused by lighting? Reverend Riley and his dog were just fine.
I figure this is just like that, nothin' to worry about

            (after they exit, WILLIAM sinks into the nearest chair
            and lets out a heavy breath. There is a clap of thunder)

WILLIAM

What am I going to do? I told myself that I was going to come in here
and tell her the truth, tell her everything... but now... how can I? She's
so worried about Peter and I went and reassured her that everything
was going to be okay... how could I do that when I know that
everything won't be, is not okay... I need to tell her the truth but how
can I? I don't think I can look her in the eyes and tell her the truth.
Maybe I should just write her a letter and leave it for her to find, then I
won't have to face her...
            (WILLIAM looks around for a minute and then grabs
            a piece of paper from the bar, he takes a pen out of his
            pocket)
Dear Fannie. Sorry that I couldn't tell you this in person, but I didn't
know what to say.
            (A clap of thunder, PETER enters silently)
You are my best friend, and I won't wanna do anything to hurt ya, but I
can't keep this a secret any longer/

PETER

Hey Will! Whatcha workin on?

WILLIAM

What nothin' Peter?! Where've you been

PETER

I've been around, but seriously whatcha writin?

WILLIAM

Oh uh, its nothin

PETER

Ah come on Will- it just me, let me see it

(PETER snaches the note)

WILLIAM

Hey- Peter. Give it back

PETER

Why? It about me

WILLIAM

Not everythin is 'bout you/

PETER

Oh but this is/

WILLIAM

No. it not. come on. give it back. Give it back-
                    (finally getting the note back)
It's none a ya business/

PETER

Watcha writtin to Fannie?

WILLIAM

What? Ah it nothin

PETER

If it nothin, show me

WILLIAM

Peter seriously, it no big deal

PETER

No big deal? What's goin on with you and Fannie?

WILLIAM

Peter it's nothing damn calm down

PETER

Calm down? You tryin to steal Fannie? Is that what that is about?

WILLIAM

Peter no 'course not. I just... I gotta tell her what happened, she gotta know the truth, she's worried sick about ya and I know what happened

PETER

Oh so you're gunna tell your version of the story, and what? Make me look like the bad guy

WILLIAM

No I'm gunna tell her it like it happened. And what you mean? I ain't the bad guy here

PETER

You ain't the bad guy? So you sayin I am?

WILLIAM

It was an accident and I never meant to hurt you/ or Fannie-

PETER

Well it's too late for that now ain't it?

WILLIAM

It wasn't just me! You agreed to it! I did nothin' wrong. Nothin'/

PETER

Keep telling yourself that/

WILLIAM

I will. This is your fault as much as/ it is mine

PETER

See you always gonna make it out to be my fault/

WILLIAM

This wouldn'ta happened if you could just learn to let thing go/

PETER

Let things go? You were movin in on my girlfri/end

WILLIAM

For the last time I was not/

PETER

And now you're gunna make it out like it was all my doin. I thought we swore we'd be keepin it a secret. Guess I know what your word is good for.

WILLIAM

I'd only be tellin Fannie- She deserves to know… but Peter you really should be the one to tell her

PETER

Me tell her? And what exactly would I say?

WILLIAM

I don't know but it'd sound better comin from you

PETER

I can't… I can't tell her, she'll hate me

WILLIAM

She'll be heartbroken but she could never hate ya

PETER

You don't know that… I can't tell her… I just can't

(PETER exits)

WILLIAM

Peter- come on-

(WILLIAM follows after PETER leaving the door
open. Another clap of thunder and then FANNIE
enters)

FANNIE

Breakfast's ready, we're eating in the kitchen…

(FANNIE looks around for a beat before noticing the
open door. It is pouring outside. Slowly closes the
door. And looks around the bar again. Lights fade to
black)

SCENE 3

(Lights up on PETER and WILLIAM. They stand
back to back in an isolated pool of light. It is raining.
They walk three paces away from each other in sync.
A beat after the third step they quickly turn around
and shoot, almost immediately WILLIAM falls to the
ground. A scream from offstage. Blackout)

SCENE 4

(Lights up on Nancy's Bar. RICHARD is setting up
the tables while NANCY polishes some glasses at the
bar. GEORGE enters the bar shaking off a wet
umbrella.)

GEORGE

Evening, is there a place I can store my umbrella?

NANCY

Leave it there by the door, Richard'll get it. Richard did'ya remember to
take the towels off the line?

RICHARD

Oh no… I forgot

NANCY

Well get on and do that now, it rainin again

> (RICHARD runs offstage, then runs back onstage,
> trips, and takes GEORGE's umbrella and sets it in a
> bucket by the door. He then runs offstage. GEORGE
> finds this amusing. NANCY does not)

GEORGE

Yours?

NANCY

Yes, my only child. Some days I'm not sure if im lucky or unlucky cause a' that

GEORGE

Why would it be unlucky?

NANCY

Not sure if you've noticed, but this is a very college town, and there ain't a lot of children his age 'round here. And those that are his age have parents that don't approve of a mother that basically runin' a bar while raisin' a child. They don't quite think it's right.

GEORGE

Now what wouldn't be right about that? Seems a fairly decent bar by the looks of it

NANCY

You've ain't been in here but two minutes how'd ya figure it's decent?

GEORGE

You tellin me it's not?

NANCY

Oh no it's a quaint little place, I was just inquiring about the nature of yer judgement as it was given so rapidly.

GEORGE

Oh I'm a good judge of character, and this bar has quite a bit of it

NANCY

Why yes it does, now what can I get for ya?

GEORGE

I'll have a whiskey

NANCY

Alright one whisky coming right up

GEORGE

So you run this place all by yourself?

NANCY

Well, technically my husband is supposed to be the one runnin' it, but he ain't ever come here but to drink the free booze. 'eryone know its me thats keepin this place afloat, And I do what I can

GEORGE

Ah well, this place seems kinda empty, is it always like this?

NANCY

Oh no, I reckon it's the weather keepin most people inside, that or the looming exams

GEORGE

Ah if I remember my college days it's likely more the weather keepin people away

NANCY

On nights like these we'll get a few stragglers like yerself, what brings ya out tonight?

GEORGE

I'm actually looking for someone, my nephew, his family ain't heard from him in a while and they're getting a bit anxious bout it. I had business in the area and offered to check in on him, problem is no one round here seems to know a thing about him

NANCY

Anything you do hear is likely gunna be nothin but gossip with maybe a tenth of truth mixed in ever so slightly. Who ya lookin for?

GEORGE

His name's Peter Dromgoole

NANCY

Peter, peter, peter- he's been quite popular today, everyone seems to be lookin for him, betting you're arrival had something to do bout that

GEORGE

You knew I was in town lookin?

NANCY

News travels fast in a town like this, there ain't nothin I don't know about what's goin on here

GEORGE

Well what have you heard about me?

(GEORGE motions for another drink. NANCY pours him one)

NANCY

Nothin that I know to be true, just that you're in town lookin for your nephew

GEORGE

And? So you know what happened to Peter?

NANCY

Oh I know what people say happened to Peter-but that it. don't know what parts are true

GEORGE

And? What are people sayin? All I can get are platitudes about what a great guy he was but I know when people are tellin me half truths, there's somethin they're not saying.

NANCY

Well Peter is always gettin into trouble with somebody or another, and he's not at all serious bout school, not that he didn't have his good qualities but he was always causing alotta trouble that people weren't always too keen about

GEORGE

I'm well acquainted with the... Finer points of his personality, I just want to know where he's run off to

NANCY

I heard all sorts of rumors, most of them claiming he's up and left without tellin a soul, but I know Peter, he wouldn't have left without no goodbye, he had many faults but he would have stopped and said farewell.

GEORGE

And what about Fannie, that professor's daughter? Do you know where I can find her?

NANCY

Sir, I tell you this with all due respect, but you leave that poor girl alone. If she knew anything, I'd know it too. All you'd be doin is upsetting her and makin her worry over probably nothin

GEORGE

Mrs. I respect that, but she might know where Peter's gone and I gotta follow every lead I get.

NANCY

All right, All right- But don't you dare upset her

GEORGE

I will do my best not to, another one?

(NANCY pours another glass of whiskey, the door opens and JAMES enters. Not at all prepared for the rain but seemingly missed the worst of the weather)

NANCY

Why James, what a pleasant surprise. Twice in one day what an occurrence, what can I get for ya?

JAMES

A whisky please Mrs. Nancy. Good evening Senator Dromgoole.

NANCY

Senator? I guess that explains the, um excellent character judgement

GEORGE

Well, it'sa requirement in my profession- politicians ain't always as trustworthy and honest as you'd want 'em to be

NANCY

Don't I know it, James I'm outta whiskey I'm gonna grab some from the back I'll be right back hun

(NANCY exits)

JAMES

How are you Senator?

GEORGE

I'm doing quite alright James and how about yourself?

JAMES

Doing well bout done with this semester

GEORGE

Ah yes, I heard about the exams

JAMES

Had the last of 'em today, now just waitin for the results

GEORGE

Smart boy like yourself, I am sure you'll do just fine. Have you heard anything from Peter?

JAMES

Sir, like I said dis morning I haven't seen him in quite some time and-

GEORGE

I've been hearing that he has left town

(RICHARD re-enters)

JAMES

His things are still in our room- but I ain't seen him. It is quite possible he's been staying elsewhere, but I wouldn't really know where

GEORGE

Surely he must have said something to someone, that he was planning on leavin' and where he was going?

JAMES

I'm sorry sir-

RICHARD

(quietly)

I 'eard something….

JAMES

Richard, what do you mean you heard something?

RICHARD

Mama says I shouldn't say thing about Peter that ain't true

GEORGE

It alright son, what you heard could help us figure out what where Peter went

RICHARD

But mama says that lies make it more difficult to figure out the truth.

GEORGE

Well… sometimes that is the case, but usually the lies have a bit of truth in 'em. And that bit of truth is what we need to find the whole truth. Does that make sense?

RICHARD

Ummmmmm No.

JAMES

What he's trying to say is you can tell us what you know and we won't get mad if it is a rumor and not true, cause we want to know the rumors too.

RICHARD

Okay well I heard that- wait
> (runs to the door that leads to the kitchen listens intently for a moment and then runs back to GEORGE and JAMES)

I hadda make sure mama wasn't comin back. See she don't like it when I tells rumors

GEORGE

Of course, now what did you hear?

RICHARD
> (running over the words)

I 'eard that another guy was interested in Fannie and they got into dis huge argument about it. Though maybe it wasn't 'bout Fannie cause they argued all the time, Not Fannie and Peter but Peter and the other guy. But I 'eard that Peter challenged him to a duel or maybe he challenged Peter I don't know... But anyway they were gonna duel and they decided to meet at like this special rock in the woods. Tommy said that when you duel you gotta stand back to back and then you suddenly turn and shoot the other person. But you gotta turn at the same time? How do ya know when to turn if you ain't facing each other? Oh but Tommy said that Susans older brother said that Peter died in the duel. Well Susan said that he died in Fannie's arms, who was watchin the duel. But if he died wouldn't there be a funeral?

GEORGE

Do you know who the opponent was?

RICHARD

If he got shot does that mean the other guy got shot? Did the other guy die too? Is that why there ain't a funeral. Tommy's brother said Fannie couldn't a been their cause if she loved Peter she wouldn't a let him get killed when he got shot, she would have gotten someone to save him. Susan said she didn't tell anyone cause she loved the other guy too and didn't want him to be in trouble. But Tommy's brother said Fannie wasn't there. Oh I also hear tell that they were buried under dat special rock. So that means someone else had to be there, to bury 'em ya know? Tommy said it was likely their seconds who buried 'em and they don't wanna get in trouble now cause dueling is bad. What's a second? And why would they duel? When Tommy and I fight it's just for fun, is dueling fun? Is that why they did it? It doesn't sound like it would be fun, Do ya always die from duels-

GEORGE

Do you know if there is anyone who might actually know about who else was supposedly involved in this duel

RICHARD

I don't know… oh! Daddy said he seen Peter and um… I don't 'member his name but he's good friends with Peter and Fannie arguing outside the bar about somein' maybe it was that guy

GEORGE

Oh great
                 (quickly downs the rest of his drink)
I don't suppose he's gunna be in anytime soon

RICHARD

I dunno, he ain't around alot. When he does come in he goes and drinks a whoooole bottle of whiskey… then he and mama get inta fights/

GEORGE
                 (under his breath)
Does anyone in this town actually know anything.

RICHARD

I ain't supposed to know they fightin cause they think I'm asleepin- mama don't like talkin bout him she get real upset whenever he comes

(NANCY re-enters)

NANCY

Whenever who comes?

RICHARD

Oh um… no one… we aint talking about nothin… he was just askin' questions bout Peter and I was just… well I was just tellin them what Tommy told me-

NANCY

Richard- what did I tell 'bout rumors?

RICHARD

But I didn't say nothin' I was just makin a guessin… is that still a rumor

NANCY

Richard it's gettin late, it's fixin to be time for bed

RICHARD

Aw ma! But I wanna know what happened to Peter

NANCY

You and everyone else in this town apparently, I don't figure we'll discover anything new tonight, and if we do I will tell you in the morning- Off to bed

RICHARD

But ma-
            (NANCY silences him with a look)
Okay… g'night Ma, g'night James

JAMES

Goodnight Richard

GEORGE

Thanks for chatting with me, have a good night

> (RICHARD exits slowly, hoping they will start talking about Peter again. NANCY waits deliberately, pouring JAMES a whiskey and GEORGE another)

NANCY

I apologize 'bout my son, He's got a wild imagination that refuses to be tempered

GEORGE

It's ain't a problem at all, though- Do you know who Peter would have a quarrel with?

JAMES

I don't know anyone/

NANCY

Peter quarrelled with almost everyone he met, but he does have some sense in him and would never have let it lead to some silly duel, much less have let himself die in that duel

GEORGE

So you knew about the duel?

NANCY

Like I said earlier, I know bout the rumors but not bout the truths

GEORGE

Well, what do you figure about dis, I spoke with Thomas Hunt before I arrived who claimed that Peter, using the name Williams, stayed with a member of his church and then left to join the army at Smithfield

> (sets the empty glass down with a flourish of finality, NANCY unconvinced pours him another)

NANCY

Peter, under the name of Williams, joined the army? How'd ya figure that out?

GEORGE

Well this woman that attends his church, claims this man Williams left buncha letters, addressed to Peter Dromgoole, behind. Now, why don't you tell me how else those letters would'a gotten there?

NANCY

Why that is a question that I don't quite have the answer to- but I still find the story unlikely

JAMES

Did you say this man went by Williams?

GEORGE

Yes! indeed, the women at the from the church claims he went by a uh John Buxton Williams

JAMES

But thats-

GEORGE

I know! So let me ask you dis, did you spend any time recently in Louisburg with Peter's letter?

JAMES

Of course not, I've been studying practically non-stop of the past month, so much so that I ain't even realize it'a been so long since I last seen Peter

NANCY

Let me get this straight, you are claiming that Peter joined the military under James's name because some women has a bunch of Peter's letters?

GEORGE

Ain't you so adamant that he ain't duel

NANCY

Of course he ain't die in no duel, but he also woulda left without sayin no goodbye.

GEORGE

So if he aint die in a duel. And he aint join the military- whatta you figure did happen

JAMES

Why Mrs. Nancy? Didn't you say earlier that Peter left some mail here?
Maybe the letters will tell us what he was thinkin

GEORGE

You gotta Peter's letters? Give'em here

NANCY

Well I was waitin to give 'em to Peter, but I suppose if you're his family
there's no harm in ya seein 'em.
                    (NANCY searches for a moment. With a sigh)
Well they ain't here, but the mail I was gunna get posted today is...
Richard!

RICHARD
                    (entering sheepishly. He did not go to bed)
Yes mama

NANCY

Did you forget to post today's mail?

RICHARD

No! I swears I grabbed the letters by the cashbox like always and/

NANCY

This is the mail I wanted posted today, looks like you went and posted
Peter's mail instead

RICHARD

Oh... sorry mama

NANCY

Well there ain't nothin we can do bout it now

RICHARD

So Peter joined the military! Dat's so cool! Do ya think he gonna be
fightin the Indians?

NANCY

Richard! What did I say 'bout rumors

RICHARD

But-

NANCY

But nothin, get to bed you and I mean bed, and if I heard that you've
been tellin people about Peter and military, I swear to god/

GEORGE

Don't be to hard on the boy, it just a bit a gossip it all natural and ain't
hurt anyone

NANCY

It hurts quite a few people when it is vicious rumors that are spread
with no recourse

GEORGE

They ain't no big deal, don't worry 'bout it 'ichard, Gossip is natural
and there's ain't nothing you can do to stop it/

NANCY

You can stop spreadin the lies- if you don't know it's true don't be
treatin it as fact. Richard, Bed.

RICHARD

Yes mama, g'night everybody

(RICHARD exits solemnly)

GEORGE

'nother round

NANCY

Of course

(she fills both glasses, and, after a beat, pours one for
herself)

JAMES

Oh no, I'm quite alright

GEORGE

Nonsense, it's on me

JAMES

No, one is enough for me

GEORGE

Well if you insist

> (Quickly finishes his whiskey and takes JAMES's glass.
> Downs it. Motions for NANCY to pour him another.
> She does.)

NANCY

Well Senator, whatcha planning to do now?

GEORGE

Please, call me George-
> (GEORGE has picked up the bottle of whiskey and is
> serving himself at this point)
and I ain't sure, If Peter has run off then there's ain't much I can do
'bout it. No one 'round here knows nothin. I suppose I could inquire
with Fannie and um James no not james uh I don't think I ever got his
name your husband? Is he your husband? I don't know, but to be
perfectly honest this is all very tiresome. I am sure Peter will come to
his senses soon and write to his family or somethin'

NANCY

Yes I'm sure he will, and until then?

GEORGE

Well I guess I'll just write to his father and tell him that, everyone
thought quite highly of Peter, and uh no one heard 'bout a quarrel but
he's disappeared-gone, poof. Nothin more I can do here, I gotta get
back to Virginia soon.

NANCY

You'll stop looking for him just like that?

GEORGE

Well you the one so adamant that he did not disappear so it means he
gotta be 'round here somewhere
                    (Looks around the bar as if PETER will just appear)
I am sure he's just enjoying the sunshine and the nice weather and he's
probably gunna be comin back when it's cold outside or somethin

JAMES

Are you sure he's gonna come back

NANCY

James!

JAMES

I know I don't want to believe it either, but he's left his belongings, not
told anyone anything and has apparently joined the army under my
name or died in some silly duel.

GEORGE

Oh his things- I guess I should take care of those… Do you think they
are terribly important? I don't want to have to deal with the additional
luggage on the train… Maybe I can only take what is important and oh-
we're out of whiskey

JAMES

I can take care of his affects Senator

GEORGE

Oh well that'd be ah that quite nice of you. And it would save me all
that trouble

                    (tries to pour another glass forgetting he is out of
                    whiskey. NANCY and JAMES exchange a look.)

NANCY

Well it sounding like the weather has cleared up a bit, so you won't get
drenched on the way home

GEORGE

Oh ya think so? that's nice. never did like the rain

JAMES

Well I gunna take this chance to head home. Sentor, would you like me to walk with you to your accommodations?

GEORGE

Why that would be wonderful, It's been quite sometime since I been here last and nothing looks the same anymore. It all done change. Do ya think it's wet outside? Oh and, here ya go

> (GEORGE puts some money on the counter, and starts to leave.)

NANCY

Don't forget your umbrella sir

GEORGE

Oh yes of course, thank you thank you. Uh well- have a good night

NANCY

You as well

(GEORGE exits)

Good night to you too James, get home safe. Oh and James, you'll tell me if you hear anythin about Peter right?

JAMES

Of course, Good night Mrs. Nancy...but you're probably right and it ain't nothin

(JAMES exits)

NANCY

I hope you're right, I really hope that you're right

> (NANCY takes a bottle of liquor from under the bar, pours herself a glass and sits at one of the tables. She has a few sips and seems lost in thought, the light slowly fades)

SCENE 5

(Lights up on an isolated pool of light where PETER
and WILLIAM stand back to back. It is raining. They
walk three paces away from each other in sync. A beat
after the third step they quickly turn around and shoot,
almost suddenly both PETER and WILLIAM fall to
the ground. FANNIE screams and runs into the light.
She checks the pulse on PETER first, he is not
responsive. WILLIAM coughs weakly, FANNIE runs
to his side)

FANNIE

William? William? What happened?

WILLIAM

We got in an argument, I --- offended him and so --- he --- wanted to
duel--- I didn't think that ---- I did not --- want to hurt him --- is he---?

FANNIE

I don't… I don't know…you're bleeding! Can you stand?

(FANNIE tries to help WILLIAM up, she is
unsuccessful)

WILLIAM

Don't bother with me--- check on--- Pe-- Peter--- he--- has--- to be---
alright

FANNIE

William… I think… I don't… William? William!
(She drags WILLIAM closer to PETER, and props
him up so he is leaning against her.)
William stay awake… I can't… I can't lose both of you!

WILLIAM

It's okay- you'll be okay

FANNIE

But- I love you, I love both of you, I can't live without you guys

(FANNIE takes PETER's hand and puts her other arm for securely around WILLIAM)

WILLIAM
I--- loved you both too-- you will--- be--- okay--- I--- promise

(WILLIAM reaches to grab FANNIE's hand where it is holding PETER's. His wheezing subsides until all that can be heard are FANNIES sobs which soon also fade away. A boom of thunder is heard with a strike of lighting. A brief blackout and we are back in the bar. NANCY bolts awake. She looks around the bar and the rain can be heard from outside. RICHARD enters sleepily)

RICHARD
Mama? I can't sleep the thunder is scary and I had a bad dream

NANCY
It's okay dear go on back upstairs, I'll be up in a minute

(RICHARD exits. NANCY takes a deep steadying breath, stands and returns the liquor to the bar, then grabs the glasses and exits into the kitchen)

NANCY
He is fine, it is just a rumor, just a rumor

(as the lights fade there is another bolt of lighting and thunder that briefly illuminates FANNIE, WILLIAM, and PETER, pale and holding hands before a complete blackout)

(END OF PLAY)

Kiss Fell

A One-Act Play by Sorcha de Faoite

Who are our people? It's a strange question when you really stop and think about it. Our friends, colleagues, members of the bi - weekly book club or the gals we meet for brunch on a Sunday. What do all these groups have in common? We choose (for the most part) who we get to spend our time with as adults. Before the grand old age of eighteen our social circles are largely out of our control.

Think of all the extra curricular activities you took part in as a child and the people you interacted with. For a time they were your "folk". Then you move on and you forget or you try to.

While on a semester abroad from Ireland, I attended the Duke VS Chapel Hill basketball game in February and was reminded of my years playing basketball from the age of eight to eighteen. For everyone on the team, our lives revolved around and were shaped by basketball. In those ten years of change and madness, basketball was the only constant. It was both strangely comforting and restrictive. With underage competitive sports you're placed into a group and told to work seamlessly together. You gather every week so adults can shout at you to throw a ball into a hoop better. Is this how you find your people?

The five girls in this short play are in a very important game. They were my "folk" and I hope they're doing well.

- Sorcha de Faoite

Cast of Characters

Anna
Bríd
Cathy
Dara
Eilish

Coach (played by Cathy)
Mum (played by Anna)

Kiss Fell

AT RISE:

Basketball court with two benches upstage

COACH
Okay Girls, tomorrow is the big day! Rest up, that means no straining yourself tonight ok! I dunno put on some Hannah Montana or something and chill out?

DARA
We're U16 not U10 Coach.

COACH
Right, yeah well I dunno whatever ye do to relax... do that ok? This is serious stuff tomorrow lads, ye know that. I don't want another silver medal. It is vital to my - *ahem* **our** reputation that we win the final tomorrow! Think of the glory when ye come home as CHAMPIONS!

Cheers from the girls.

COACH
Right, head home now and I'm dead serious. We don't need any random injuries or illnesses before the game alright?

Nods from the girls.

COACH
Right, ye can head home so!

Girls begin to run out.

COACH shouts after

Get some sleep!

COACH *phone rings, he answers*
Shtory!? Where are ye? I'll be there in ten, get me a Heineken will ye?

He leaves
BRÍD is alone on stage
She takes out her phone and calls someone

BRÍD
So what'll it be today? Finished in an hour? So you'll be here in what
hour and a half? No it's fine, it's fine I've my homework with me. No
it's not cold. I was running around there so I'm roastin'.
No I'm not asking the girls for a lift,they're gone anyways. I'll just
practice a bit. The hall isn't locked til like 9 anyways. Mom, it's fine!
Seriously! I'll see you in an hour and *checks time* twenty nine minutes.
Bye, bye, bye, bye love ya too, bye, bye.

Sound of a car starting up

_____

In a car (made of the bench)
DARA gets in, closes door
MUM begins driving

MUM
How was practice?

DARA
It was grand, yeah.

MUM
All ready for tomorrow?

DARA
I suppose, yeah.

MUM
How long is it now?

DARA

What?

                    MUM

Since you started.

                    DARA

What, started playing?

                    MUM

Yeah.

                    DARA

I dunno, like, six years?

                    MUM

But you were with the other girls for a year before.

                    DARA

So seven?

                    MUM

Time Flies.

                    DARA

It does, yeah.

Pause

                    MUM

How long are we going to keep doing this?

                    DARA

What do you mean? (I know what she means)

                    MUM

It's been six years and every week it's a struggle to get you here.

                    DARA

No it's not (it is).

                    MUM

Dara, cut the shit now.

                    DARA
(Here we go)

                    MUM
Every week you've some illness or injury that magically appears before
a game or training. The other mums have been talking and -

                    DARA
Clearly you care what they think so.

                    MUM
Don't be putting words in my mouth Dara, that's not what I said at all.

                    DARA
(Why won't she just say it)

                    MUM
What are we doing out here if you -

                    DARA
(Just say I can quit)

                    MUM
It's getting ridiculous.

                                        They've arrived
                        DARA opens door, just before she leaves

                    DARA
Thanks for picking me up.

                                        Motions to close door
                        Before it closes, EILISH catches it and jumps in
                                        MUM starts driving

                    EILISH

Hey Mum, sorry I'm late! Coach was trying to inspire us with some big speech. You'd think he'd be better at that by now!

MUM

How was practice?

EILISH

It was great! Look.

She pulls up one side of her shorts to reveal a sizeable bruise

MUM

Jesus Eilish!

EILISH

Mad, isn't it. Must've been there for a while but I only noticed it there. I wonder when I got it?

MUM

Was it the time you tripped over the bench at half time?

EILISH

Nah that wasn't thaaat sore.

MUM

Or when that girl accidentally kicked you when she fell?

EILISH

It doesn't really look like a footprint though. Wait I think I know, it was when Anna got really mad and threw the ball.

MUM

What?

EILISH

yeah it was last week I think? She kept missing her three pointers.

MUM

You didn't tell me that.

EILISH
I forgot, looks like my leg didn't though! What's for dinner? I'd murder a chicken kiev.

MUM
Eilish do you think tomorrow might be it?

EILISH
I hope so, I'd do anything to win and I heard that there might be a scout from the National Squad there -

MUM
No Eilish, I mean tomorrow might be your last game.

EILISH
What? Well even if I don't make the team I'll still have next year.

MUM
Eilish, I think you need to quit.

EILISH
What? You're messin.

MUM
I'm not. I don't think this… environment.. is good for you.

They've arrived

MUM
Look we'll talk about it again. I just want you to be prepared that tomorrow could be your last game.

Pause

MUM
Come in and have your dinner.

EILISH

Will you still come to the game?

MUM

Of course. Lord above though if it gets down to the wire my nerves
will be gone!

She goes offstage
As EILISH goes

EILISH

It won't, we've been working extra hard this year, there's no way -

Sound of a whistle
The girls run onto the bench
They're exhausted

ANNA

It's down to the wire.

EILISH

It's 20 seconds left on the clock.

ANNA

It's 21.74 seconds left on the clock.

EILISH

It's 20 seconds.

ANNA

21.74.

EILISH

What are you doing?

ANNA

It's 21.74.

EILISH

It's more dramatic if it's 20.

ANNA

It's more correct if it's 21.74.

Pause

EILISH
It's **21.74** seconds left on the clock of an important game that none of us will remember the name of in ten years -

Daggers from ANNA and BRÍD

DARA
That **most** of us won't remember the name of in ten years
We're level but we wouldn't be if

She hesitates, she doesn't want to say it

CATHY
I hadn't missed my free throws

ANNA
Look it usually wouldn't be a huge deal but not only is this THE final but…
whispers the scout for the national team is here!

All the girls look out into the audience.
ANNA and BRÍD begin to stretch very obviously, exaggerated.
*EILISH tries but she can't **quite** touch her toes.*
DARA rolls her eyes.
CATHY is miming how to take a free throw, oblivious.
Sound of whistle.

CATHY stands up and crouches in front of girls, becoming their Coach.

COACH
Missed your free throws again but we'll talk about that at practice.

Over the course of the following, COACH draws a play on a small whiteboard and speaks as though he is describing the logistics.

We've got to focus on the next 20 seconds, block everything out of your mind OK? Try and steal the ball. Anna, you're going to drive the ball down the court as fast as you can, I should not have gone out last night. Get to the basket and draw that foul. Six pints was a big mistake. And don't get me started on the taxi home. This is our home court, we have the advantage. You call horns if you have to ok? That'll throw them off. Why didn't she pick up last night? I thought things were going well between us, I know it was late but still. And nothing from her this morning. When that screen comes up, you need to brush shoulders with her otherwise they could call foul and we CANNOT let them get the ball again. I should've fucked off to Australia with the rest of the lads but I'm here on my Sunday morning. And be ready for the side pass if it comes yer way. Dara… Cathy I'm looking at ye do ye hear me?

Everyone nods.
The play is drawn on the whiteboard.

COACH

Right, hands in!

They do so.

COACH

I'm incredibly lonely! Let's go, come on girls, we can do this!

COACH sits down and then runs on as C.
The girls walk onto the court.
While walking and getting into position.

ANNA

Just leave it off, alright.

EILISH

Why didn't you tell any of us?

ANNA

Now is not the time Eilish!

BRÍD

What's going on?

ANNA

Nothing.

EILISH

She went on a date.

CATHY

So, what's the big deal?

EILISH

It was with Sean!!!

ANNA

Eilish!

DARA

What, Sean on the rugby team?

CATHY

Wait but isn't that -

BRÍD

My brother?!

Sound of a whistle.
Dialogue gets quicker.

ANNA

I was going to tell you.

BRÍD

And when were you thinking?

ANNA

Definitely not in the middle of the most important game of our lives!

DARA *to herself*

Dramatic

BRÍD

How long?

ANNA

Jesus they're about to pass it in, can we not just -

Dialogue is pretty frantic by now.

BRÍD

How long?

ANNA

Not long!

EILISH

That's a lie, it's been going on ages!

ANNA

How would you know?

EILISH

I saw ye at the cinema the last day.

CATHY

What film did ye see?

BRÍD

Jesus cathy, I don't care about that. Did ye… shift?

The rest of the girls react.

ANNA

Oh my God, the ref is about to pass it to her can we -

BRÍD

Fucking hell, ye did!

CATHY

That's mad.

ANNA *deflecting, looking for any way out*
What, are ya a frigid or something?

CATHY
So what if I've never kissed a boy.

ANNA
Oh my God you are a frigid!

CATHY
It's not a big deal, not everyone has kissed someone!

Sound of a whistle, the ball is passed in.

DARA
I can't believe I'm saying this but I think we should focus right now!

All reluctantly agree.

EILISH
Jesus their point guard can't dribble for shit. She just sticks her arse into me when I'm defending. But the beauty of basketball is that it's a non contact sport so even if she wanted to -

EILISH jerks her head back and falls to the floor.

All exclaim.

EILISH *clutching her nose*
She elbowed me?! What the fuck? Ref?!

EILISH stays on the ground.
The girls run over to her.
CATHY examines the floor.
DARA hovers in the back, concerned.
BRÍD examines her face.

Sound of a whistle.

CATHY

Is there blood?

DARA

Y'alright?

BRÍD

I don't think it's broken.

EILISH

I think it's ok, it's sore like.

Sound of a whistle.

ANNA

The ref wants to start up again.

CATHY

Oh you are bleeding!

BRÍD

What, I don't see it?

EILISH

I thought you said it wasn't broken?

BRÍD

I said I don't **think** it's broken

EILISH

Well what do you think then?

Sound of a whistle.

ANNA

Guys there's only -ten- seconds left, we -

CATHY

Don't put your head back, it'll bleed **into your brain** -

DARA

Will I get the first aider?

CATHY

What if she can't breathe?

EILISH, *getting worried*

What do you mean?

BRÍD

Stop that, she'll be grand, you'll be grand!

DARA

So the first aider is at the lads game.

BRÍD

Course.

Sound of a whistle.

EILISH

Where's Mum?

The girls look into the crowd for their Mums.

DARA

They're probably outside.

BRÍD

Will I go out?

Sound of a whistle.

CATHY

I could do with the fresh air.

DARA

I'll go, you stay with her.

Sound of a whistle.

BRÍD

I'll get some tissue.

ANNA

Will you just get up!

Everyone freezes.
DARA is nearly at the door.
BRÍD is about halfway to the door.
EILISH is still clutching her nose.
Even CATHY is shocked.
Silence.

ANNA

We've only got - ten - seconds left, just take your free throws!

Sound of a whistle.
EILISH gets up, the girls get into position for free throws.
First one is a miss.
Second one in, cue louder **screams** *from the crowd.*
A timer of **10 seconds** *flashes on the stage.*
It counts down, the screams get louder and louder.
00:00 *shows on stage.*
At <u>zero</u>, *the girls celebrate just as* **wildly** *as the crowd,*
forgetting everything that just happened.
Euphoria *fills the stage for a brief moment.*
The lights fade down as the girls run off, ANNA hangs back.

ANNA stretches.
Enter BRÍD in different training gear.

BRÍD

Hey.

ANNA

What are ya doing here?

BRÍD

Couldn't miss the last session to be fair.

ANNA

You didn't hear?

BRÍD

What?

ANNA

Trainin's canceled.

BRÍD

What, since when?

ANNA

Coach went on a bender after we won, tried on someones high heels in the pub and

Motions breaking something with her hands.

BRÍD

Jesus, is he ok?

ANNA

Well, no like but he'll live.

BRÍD

Why didn't I hear?

ANNA

Dunno, I got a text, did you or your Mam not get one?

BRÍD

No, I don't - Wait, if you knew training was cancelled what are you still doing here?

Pause.

ANNA

Mam and Dad were having a shouting match, said I'd leave it to them to decide the winner. They didn't know trainin' was cancelled.

BRÍD

Oh -

ANNA

It's grand, just needed a bit of space.

BRÍD

I didn't know that -

ANNA

S'grand.

BRÍD

Why didn't the girls come, would've been nice to have one last hurrah before next year.

ANNA

They quit.

BRÍD

What?

ANNA

They quit. All of them. Dara, Eilish, Cathy. All quit.

BRÍD

Fuck off.

ANNA

I'm serious. They left.

BRÍD

Why?

ANNA

Didn't say although Mam seems to think it may have something to do
with my anger issues.

Pause.

BRÍD

But we won't have enough to make a team.

ANNA

I know.

Pause.

BRÍD

No more games.

Pause.

ANNA

Yeah.

Pause.

BRÍD

Look since you're here, I have something to tell you before you hear it
somewhere else. I made it.

ANNA *oblivious*

Made what?

BRÍD

The National squad.

ANNA stops.

BRÍD

I didn't want to tell you cause I know you said you hadn't heard
anything but they said they'd be announcing it online today and I didn't
want you to see and think I didn't tell you on purpose.

Pause.

BRÍD

Not that I'm saying that you didn't get on the team because maybe they
just haven't told you yet, has your phone been on or like have you
checked -

ANNA

It's grand.

BRÍD

What is?

ANNA

It's fine, I didn't make the team. It's fine.

Pause.

BRÍD

Are you sure you're ok?

No response from ANNA.

BRÍD

Because it'd be fairly understandable if you weren't... ok.

ANNA

I just don't know what I'm going to do now.

BRÍD

You can always try again next year.

ANNA

How am I supposed to practice if we don't even have this team.

> **BRÍD**

You'll think of something! I'm always around if you want someone to
do drills with.

> **ANNA**

Am I supposed to be flattered?

> **BRÍD**

What?

> **ANNA**

Cause you got on the National Squad, you'll practice with me like I'm
some sort of charity case?

> **BRÍD**

Jesus Anna I didn't mean it like that.

> **ANNA**

I don't need your help.

> **BRÍD**

Fine you don't need my help, but a congrats or well done would be
nice.

> **ANNA**

For what?

> **BRÍD**

Are you serious? For getting on the fucking team. Maybe you're too self
absorbed to say Good job to me but you know damn well if the roles
were reversed, I wouldn't have flipped the story back to me in an
instant.

> *BRÍD goes to leave.*

> **ANNA**

I'm sorry!
I'm happy for you, you deserve it.

> **BRÍD**

Thank you.

ANNA

You work harder than anyone, well apart from Eilish maybe.

BRÍD

I can't believe she quit.

ANNA

Yeah, but she might get a free nose job so there's that.

Pause.

ANNA

Sean ended things.

BRÍD

Good.

ANNA laughs.

BRÍD

What? You're too good for him. The two points of his personality are rugby and his Honda Civic.

ANNA laughs.

ANNA

You're right. He also can't drive without his Mum so that made for some awkward dates.

BRÍD

D'ya know he failed his test?

ANNA

Seriously?

BRÍDs' phone rings.
She answers.

BRÍD

Hey Mum, yeah it was cancelled. Did you not see the text or somethin'? Yeah I know you can't pick me up. Ok grand so. Hope work is ok!

Love ya, bye.

She hangs up.

ANNA
D'ya not have a lift home?

BRÍD
I usually hang back, Mum finishes work after we finish training but Dad is at the shop so he's swingin' round.

ANNA
How long do you wait, usually?

BRÍD
Like an hour.

ANNA
An hour? And you never told us?

BRÍD
Ye all live the other way, I wasn't going to ask ye to go in the other direction.

ANNA
You should've.

Pause.

BRÍD
At least I got the extra practice in.

ANNA
You're not wrong there.

BRÍDs' phone rings, she answers it.

BRÍD *on the phone*
Ok, I'll be right out.

Pause.

BRÍD *on the phone:*
Annas' still here, is there any chance we could give her a lift?

ANNA motions to protest.

BRÍD *to ANNA*
Are you sure?

ANNA
I could do with the extra practice.

BRÍD *on the phone*
Actually, it's ok. I'll be out in a minute!

She hangs up.

BRÍD
I better run.

ANNA
Go for it.

As she's leaving.

ANNA
Congrats again!

As she's leaving.

BRÍD
Thanks!

*ANNA stands alone on stage. The sound of a gymnasium door closing.
The lights go off, one by one like they would in a gym with a similar
sound effect playing alongside.*

The End.

Ain't That Just The Way

A One-Act Play by Sam Bible-Sullivan

My family history lies in the southern mountains. Both of my parents can trace their lineage to the southern Appalachians, and my mom was born and mostly raised in the Arkansas Ozarks. Thus, my parents weren't surprised when the Western North Carolina Mountains called to them. My family moved to Asheville when I was three, so I grew up nestled in the Blue Ridge Mountains. It's a strange combination of folk in the WNC mountains, a sort of hodgepodge of country, hippie, artsy, working class, wayward, and stoner. A few decades back, these groups had more distinction, more separation, but after a couple of generations of mountain kids growing up in the mix of all these influences, the lines have gotten blurred. I think the current generation of WNC Appalachian folk embody these blurred lines. We like shooting guns and bows; we love frigid swimming holes; we'll plan a camping trip in an hour; we whittle, or paint, or poet; we drink, smoke, and trip; we rock tye dyes and pashminas and kick off our shoes whenever we can; we live life at our own, typically slower pace because no way in hell will someone tell us how quick to move; we push boundaries and experiment with the norms because the mountains don't abide by norms; we only live up to the stereotypes that are too damn fun to give up; and, I really believe we only judge you if you're just plain rude. This is the life I grew up in. This is the folk I grew up with. This is who I am. And, this is the voice, people, and mentality I tried to capture in **Ain't That Just the Way**.

- Sam Bible-Sullivan

Cast of Characters

CLYDE
RON
GEORGE
JORDAN

Setting

Suburban backyard.

Ain't That Just The Way

AT RISE:

CLYDE, GEORGE, and RON are sitting around the table stargazing. They pass a blunt amongst themselves.

CLYDE

I'm serious! Idaho is like, a super messed up state.

RON

America's like, a messed up country.

CLYDE

Yes. Yes that's totally true, but like, Idaho takes it a little further. Did you know that it's like where the most white supremacists are?

GEORGE

Makes sense.

RON

Does it make sense?

GEORGE

Yeah.

RON

How do you know?

GEORGE

'Cause it's like Idaho. Like what else does it have goin on? Besides potatoes.

CLYDE

That's what I'm sayin. It's like hella isolated over there. Especially, up at the tip, so there's no one paying attention.

RON

I don't know. I've heard it's really beautiful out there.

CLYDE

I mean, yeah, but that doesn't keep racists away.

(GEORGE takes a nice long hit from the blunt.)

GEORGE

Everybody fucks with beautiful nature.

CLYDE

True, unless there's money to be made off that beautiful nature. People fuck with money more than anything else.

(GEORGE points at CLYDE and nods in agreement while hitting the blunt again.)

RON

Yeah, obviously everybody's gonna fuck with pretty views. I wasn't sayin that would keep away nazis. I was just, just like it's got other things goin for it.

CLYDE

Well, yeah, every state's got somethin goin for it.

GEORGE

Not Delaware.

RON

The fuck *is* up with Delaware?

GEORGE

That's what I'm sayin.

CLYDE

Delaware's got crabs.

RON

Is that it?

GEORGE

I thought that was Baltimore's thing.

CLYDE

Baltimore's not a state.

GEORGE

Baltimore's a state of mind.

RON

When've you been to Baltimore?

GEORGE

Never.

RON

… word.

GEORGE

Nah, but like, Maryland. That's what's known for the crabs.

CLYDE

And Delaware.

RON

Isn't Delaware right by Maryland?

GEORGE

That'd explain the crabs.

CLYDE

Shit. Where is Delaware?

GEORGE

Wherever crabs are I guess.

CLYDE

Okay, so Delaware doesn't got shit. But hey, that's better than a stronghold of white supremacists.

RON

It's prolly got that too.

CLYDE

Well yeah, like America's got that, but I mean like it doesn't got like a blatant stronghold.

RON

How would you know? When've you been to Delaware?

GEORGE

Don't gotta go to know.

RON

Majorly disagree.

CLYDE

Nah, thassa good point. Like if it was blatant, people'd be talkin bout it. People're talkin bout Idaho.

RON

You're talkin bout Idaho.

CLYDE

Yeah, but like I read that shit on twitter, so it's not just me.

GEORGE

I'm not livin in Idaho.

RON

Did you wanna live there before?

GEORGE

No sir.

RON

Right, so like, this thing about the white supremacists didn't really turn you off Idaho. You already weren't bout livin there.

GEORGE

Yeah, but like, it hasn't helped the situation.

RON

Sure, sure, obviously, but like, this whole thing hasn't really proved that Idaho's worse than the rest of the US. Like, I feel like it's just another piece of the make up of this country.

CLYDE

Well, yeah. It's a state.

RON

Right, yes, God, I am not getting my point across. I guess, like, y'all are raggin on Idaho, but NC ain't that much better. Like, everytime I drive back to school, and back here from school, I gotta drive by that massive fuckin confederate flag. You know the one I'm talkin bout?

CLYDE

Uhhhhh. I don't think so? I drive a different route than you goin back to school.

GEORGE

I do.

RON

You've seen it George?

GEORGE

Oh hell yeah. That shit's wack as fuck but it's just a byproduct of the south.

RON

See! Now, in that sentence, you've like givin this state more of a pass then Idaho.

GEORGE

Nah, nah, nah. NC's pretty fuckin trash too.

RON

Right! The US is mostly trash, with like, little pockets of okay.

GEORGE

I mean, yeah, but that's life. Mostly trash, with little pockets of okay.

RON

What's your point there?

GEORGE

Like, you can say everything is mostly trash with little pockets of okay. Like, think about your life. Unless you've had the most definitively dope life, you're gonna say most of that shit trash with pockets of okay that, hopefully, make the trash worth it. Every part of life's like that. Except, when you're born. That shit coulda been fine, coulda not been fine, we got no clue, cause we don't remember shit until we're like four.

CLYDE

Nah, I remember shit from two.

GEORGE

Bruh, the fuck you remember from when you were two?

CLYDE

9/11.

GEORGE

No fuckin way you remember 9/11. You seriously tryna tell me you remember 9/11?

CLYDE

They told me to never forget.

GEORGE

That's OD.

RON

Really? A 9/11 joke?

CLYDE

What? Too soon?

GEORGE

See, that's how I know you don't remember that shit. Anyone, who actually remember that shit don't joke about it. Like, I got family up in NYC. That shit's still got them lowkey fucked up.

RON

It's still got the whole country lowkey fucked up. Nah, actually highkey fucked up. Y'all ever think about how much that fucked up the country? Like, that shit let the government turn this place into a surveillance state.

GEORGE

Shit dude, prolly woulda gotten there with or without it.

RON

You really think so?

GEORGE

I know so.

CLYDE

Maybe that's why I joke about it. Like, I don't know, if this sounds too fucked up, like lemme know okay?

RON

That's just never a good disclaimer.

GEORGE

Just don't say some racist shit.

CLYDE

Bruh, the fuck? I'm not gonna say racist shit.

GEORGE

Just sayin, if someone's gotta disclaim what they boutta say, nine times out of ten they're boutta say some highly racist shit.

CLYDE

Okay, yes, but like y'all, can we just agree here that none of us are ever gonna say some racist shit?

RON

Shit I'm not.

GEORGE

Same.

CLYDE

Dope, cool, but like, if any one of us does say something racist, then like we gotta get called out on it, because it's definitely coming from a place of ignorance. Like, I am not all knowing. I would say I got a pretty good intuition on how to not be an asshole, and I'd say my ma and pops did a good job raisin me, and that has not been an easy task. I am a fuckin dumbass, as we all know. But, like, yeah, I guess that's it.

RON

Bruh what?

CLYDE

Just lemme know if I'm ever on some wack shit.

GEORGE

Bruh you're always on some wack shit.

CLYDE

You know what I mean. Like, some wack, wack shit.

GEORGE

Oh imma call you out, don't worry.

CLYDE

Thank you. That's what friends are for.

GEORGE

Exactly. So, Clyde, your shoes are trash.

CLYDE

Bitch, you don't gotta call me out on shit I know. These are my trash shoes. I'm not dressin up for you fucks.

GEORGE

Damn. That's cold as hell.

RON

Do we mean nothing to you?

CLYDE

Man, y'all are the wack ones. Totally made me forget what I was gonna say. Callin me wack n' shit.

RON

You were boutta say some racist shit about 9/11.

CLYDE

Okay. Fuck off. But thank you. No racist shit, but also lemme know if this is fucked up. But, I think 9/11 is like too untouchable. Like, I know it's super sad and all, but like that tragedy has been used as an excuse for a whole lotta negative shit. Like, that whole never forget thing was like used as this battle cry for fighting back, but like fighting back against what? Terror? Okay. We decided to fight back against a concept. Dope. Let's channel all that pain and fear into vague violence. And like, all that, all that fear we had was just coming from the fact that a foreign entity was able to attack us? I get that that hadn't happened since like, Pearl Harbor, but why is it just foreign attacks we gotta remember? How about we stop forgetting all that Americans have done to other Americans? Like, lynchings still happen and people seem real willing to forget that. Or, how about we never forget what we've done to other countries? Like, how about we stop forgetting our actual history? I don't know, I just feel like you look back at so much of American history, and look at the times we're in now, and we've been

that fuckin terrorist to other countries. I mean, the CIA toppling democratically elected governments? Drone strikes? I'm just not a fan of blind patriotism and 9/11 was used as a means to fuel so much of that. And, that's carried on to this day.
Did that make sense?

                              RON
Yeah… yeah. It's like fake unity.

                            GEORGE
Fake unity?

                              RON
Yeah, like how we're supposed to all unite in moments of crisis like that. I'm not sayin people shouldn't come together as communities during times of crisis, but there's a difference between unifying against a common enemy and like coming together as a community. One's trying to destroy; the other's trying to build. One is a band-aid that makes people forget about the systemic issues that are dividing us; the other's aiming to take on those systemic issues.

                            CLYDE
Right.

                            GEORGE
Word.

                            CLYDE
Yeah, like people keep saying we're the most divided we've ever been and that we need to bridge this divide. Which like, first off, duh, stop saying shit we all already know, get into specifics. And like, second off so many people calling for this unity don't really wanna unify with everyone, most just want people to assimilate to their side, their point of view, their idea of what America is. Which like, that's not actual unity, but also I understand. I say I want to bridge the divide, but like compromising too much with people that are afraid of change… we just don't really have time for that anymore.

GEORGE

Yeah. Like, how do you reach out to someone that's so far on the other side of all that you believe? Like, how do you reach out to a bigot?

RON

Educate?

GEORGE

Yeah, but like that don't always work. Like, in order for someone to learn and grow, they gotta want to.

CLYDE

That's what I'm sayin.

GEORGE

Yeah. Like, it's easy to say, just talk it out with a nazi, but I'm not doin that. I'm sorry. We don't got time to talk shit out with nazis. We gotta move forward fast, and if people can't recognize that, I think they just gotta get left behind.

CLYDE

Yeah… Do we even really got time for unity right now?

GEORGE

Honestly? Nah. We gotta just get the shit done that's gotta get done. Universal health care, a living wage, everything related to the criminal justice system, and of course fuckin climate change. Like nothing's gonna matter if the planet dies.

CLYDE

Which is a real ass threat, and like, should be the shit that's unifying us, like climate change is a threat to the entire planet. Everyone on this planet should be coming together to fight it, but we can't even do that, so… yeah, it's just fucked.

GEORGE

Real fucked up.

RON

But, like, all that bein said… I still think we gotta try for unity. Like, shouldn't we always work towards fixin all the problems?

GEORGE

You tellin me we gotta take time from all this other shit to talk it out with nazis?

RON

I don't think we gotta take time from other shit to do that.

GEORGE

Course we do.

RON

Nah man. We really don't. 'Cause like, we're not spendin time on that other shit.

CLYDE

How so?

RON

Like, what can we, as in the three of us, as in a bunch of broke ass, middle class college kids, what can we do to fix all that other shit? Like what can we do to fix the criminal justice system?

CLYDE

Protest?

RON

But, are we protesting?

CLYDE

… nah. Only protesting I really do is say fuck 12 if I drive by a cop car.

GEORGE

Shit man, they ain't gon listen to protest.

CLYDE

You don't think they'll listen to protest?

GEORGE

They aren't listenin to protest. There's hella motherfuckers already protestin, and they ain't listenin to all them. Us joinin those ranks isn't gonna suddenly make the government decide to work towards criminal justice reform.

RON

Right. Same with the living wage, same with universal health care, same with climate change. All that stuff is too big for us. Outside of our control.

CLYDE

No, no, no. We can help the environment. Like, I'm not takin plastic bags from the grocery store anymore.

RON

That's great. But, you bought those blunt wraps right?

CLYDE

Yeah.

RON

And what was their packet made from?

CLYDE

Shit.

RON

Exactly. See, we don't got a lotta power right now to deal with that systemic shit. We don't got money, we don't got much of a platform. And even if we did, who knows if policy makers would listen?

GEORGE

Right. But how's unity not a systemic issue?

RON

I mean, that shit can get fixed just by talkin.

GEORGE

No fuckin way.

RON

I'm serious! Like, talkin with people outside of your echo chamber.
Tryin to expose your worldview to others.

GEORGE

How you gon do that?

RON

I don't know. Talkin to people I meet in my life.

GEORGE

What people? Your friends at school got different worldviews?

RON

I mean, a little.

GEORGE

Exactly. A little. You can live with a little. You can talk with a little.
How you gonna talk with a lot?

RON

A conversation couldn't hurt.

GEORGE

But what the fuck's it gon do either?

RON

Create empathy.

GEORGE

For who? You tryna empathize with confederates?

RON

Yes! And I'm tryna get them to empathize with me!

GEORGE

Never gonna happen.

RON

It could!

GEORGE

Yeah. And while you take a decade convincin him black people are people, Imma be partyin.

RON

Partyin? The fuck's that gonna do?

GEORGE

Keep me sane bitch. Look, you're right as fuck. All that big shit, we can't do nothin about. So, I'm just tryna have a good time till the world ends.

RON

Come on man. We gotta try to do what we can.

GEORGE

Oh, so you're goin out of your way to talk to confederates?

RON

Well... no. But, like, if I meet someone-

GEORGE

Where? What do you do that brings you in contact with those sorts of people?

RON

I...

GEORGE

Exactly. So you gotta take time to go out of your way to talk it out with some bigoted bitches. And you already said you aren't doin that. But, how much time you take outta your day to smoke weed?

RON

Bruh, fuck off, I don't smoke weed till I got all my shit done for the day. And like, I don't get my shit done till the evening. All the racists are at home by then.

GEORGE

Okay. How bout this summer? You been scoutin out any racists you can give an epiphany?

RON

It's the fuckin summer!

GEORGE

So you got plenty of time! But you been spendin all that time fuckin around with us. Why? Because we're way more fun to talk with then a bunch of bigots. Ron, you're doin the same thing I'm doin. You know you ain't really gonna be able to achieve shit for the world, so you tryna live in the world you've made. Tryna have the best time you can and hopin it works itself out.

RON

I...

GEORGE

And I'm tellin you that's okay! That's okay! You're a good dude Ron. I don't fuckin like people, but I love you. You're my fuckin brother. When the world's crashin down you don't go out tryna hold it up, you find your family and spend your last moments with them. That's what we're doin. We're fuckin 21; what else we gonna do?

(Pause.)

CLYDE

I've been tryna tell people at my school to not use the N word. There's way too many white ass, fuckin private school prepsters doin that shit up there.
That's somethin we can do.

RON

Yeah! That's the kinda shit I'm talkin bout!

GEORGE

Bruh, you were talkin bout singin kumbaya with the alt right!

RON

Nah man, I was talkin bout educatin!

GEORGE

That's not educatin! Maybe, *maybe*, that makes someone feel a little less comfortable bein an asshole. But they don't know why they're wrong!

RON

But-

GEORGE

That person probably still holds all their same beliefs. All callin them out does is maybe make them parade their views around less.

RON

Great! I'm okay with that. At least that's a start!

GEORGE

A start to what? You think they're gonna just decide to start educating themselves about racism in America because someone told them off for sayin the N word?

RON

Maybe they wanna know why what they did was wrong! Maybe they're sick of people being uncomfortable around them and wanna do somethin about it! Maybe that makes them go educate themselves or be open to someone educating them!

GEORGE

That's a fuck ton of maybes.

RON

At least maybes are possible solutions! All you're doin is shootin shit down.

GEORGE

All I'm doin is seein the world for how it is, seein people for how they are. You're not gonna get anyone to actually change by calling them out once for saying a slur. You should still do it because nobody needs to hear that shit, but don't act like it's somethin bigger than what it is. To get someone to actually change you have to hound them for years. You gotta put in a whole lotta time and have a whole lotta patience.

RON
So you admit it can happen!

GEORGE
Fuckin anything *can* happen! But no one wants to put the time in to fix a fuckin nazi! Not you, not me, not Clyde-

CLYDE
Whoa man, don't bring me into this.

GEORGE
Sorry. Apparently, Clyde is gonna fix nazis.

RON
Well good! Clyde should fuckin do that!

GEORGE
So you just gonna let Clyde do your dirty work?

RON
I'm not tellin Clyde to do shit! But I'll always support someone actually tryna do somethin with their life.

GEORGE
The fuck does that mean?

RON
Bruh I wasn't talkin bout you!

GEORGE
Then who the fuck were you talkin bout?

CLYDE
Ay! Both of y'all! Shut the fuck up! Damn. This is probly our last summer together. I don't want that type of energy anywhere near this time we got left. Now, having observed this heated discussion, I can say y'all are on two different parts of the same page. So Ron, admit to

George that it's highly unlikely we will be able to teach nazis to love before global warming kills us. And George, admit to Ron that you really, really, really wish it wasn't. Ron, you first.

                    RON
But, is it that unlikely?

          (GEORGE moves to start talking. CLYDE holds up a
          hand.)

                    CLYDE
Ron. Come on dude. You really think we can end that level of hate within the next 15 years?

                    RON
… yeah… yeah. George, it's really unlikely for that shit to happen.

                    GEORGE
Yeah it is… but… I really, really, really, wish it wasn't.

                    RON
Sorry dude. I got heated.

                    GEORGE
Me too.

                    RON
You know it's all love.

                    GEORGE
You already know.

          (RON and GEORGE dap each other up.)

                    CLYDE
Alright. Beef squashed?

                    RON
Yeah.

GEORGE

Beef squashed.

CLYDE

Damn. I wish it was all that easy.

GEORGE

Me fuckin too man. Me fuckin too.

RON

Maybe, one day it will be.

(They all sit in that for a moment.)

GEORGE

When y'all goin back to school?

RON

August 25th.

CLYDE

The fuck? You get to go back the 25th? Man I go back on the 19th.

RON

Guess you shoulda gone to a better school.

CLYDE

Nah, then I'd be as much of an asshole as you.

RON

Ouch. Ya cut deep Clyde, ya cut real deep.

CLYDE

Fuckin nerd.

GEORGE

Oooo, Clyde's comin for ya Ron.

RON

Bruh, I know I'm a nerd. That's not even an insult, just an observation.

GEORGE

Sounds like some nerd shit to me.

RON

Man, you're a nerd.

GEORGE

Bruh, no cap, in one of my classes last semester, like weeks into the semester, I saw this dude come in and start writin shit on the board, and I was like who the fuck is this? So I asked the guy sittin next to me, "who the fuck is that?" And this man was like, "that's the professor." So...

(They all start laughing.)

RON

That's too good oh my god.

CLYDE

I can't, like, holy shit.

(They laugh a bit longer.)

GEORGE

But yeah, not a nerd. School ain't really my thing.

RON

Shit man, I feel that. When you gotta go back?

GEORGE

The 25th.

CLYDE

What the hell??? My school's on some shit.

RON

So, it's perfect for you then?

CLYDE

Your mom's perfect for me.

GEORGE

Damnnnn, y'all chillll. Ron and I just squashed our beef.

(They all laugh.)

RON

Damn… This is really boutta be it.

CLYDE

So dramatic.

RON

Bitch you know I'm a theatre dweeb. I'm always dramatic.

CLYDE

Hahaha. True, true. But hey, you ain't the only theatre kid round here.

RON

Ha! You were in one ten minute play junior year, and the director was a student, and your co star was Claire, who you were hookin up with.

GEORGE

And you like, smoked with me before every rehearsal.

CLYDE

Y'all's point? I am still… an actor.

RON

Ohhhh. So that's why I've been in hella shows, and you've been studyin ecosystems and shit.

CLYDE

I've been preparing for a role. That's what you do right?

GEORGE

Bruh doesn't even know how to act like an actor.

(They laugh.)

RON

No, but like, for real, we all boutta be seniors. This is it.

GEORGE

Bruh, don't even talk about that shit.

RON

Haha, fair enough. I'm not tryna stress anyone out.

GEORGE

Nah. I'm not even stressed. Like, I know imma be good. I just gotta keep focused on this music.

RON

Word. Yeah, I feel that.

GEORGE

And you know-

(They all freeze as they hear the backdoor being opened. Then, JORDAN enters. Everyone cheers.)

RON

Ayyyyy! What's up man? I forgot you were comin thru, my b.

JORDAN

You good. Just glad I made it.

(JORDAN goes around and daps up RON, GEORGE, and CLYDE.)

CLYDE

You just get off work?

JORDAN

Yeah. That shit was terrible. I fuckin hate doubles. That's why I took so long. I needed to go home and shower and change and all that. Also...

(JORDAN pulls out a blunt.)

JORDAN

Needed time to roll this.

GEORGE

Ah shit. You already know.

RON

Got it already rolled and everything.

CLYDE

Shitttt, what a generous guy.

JORDAN

It's nothin. Y'all know I'm always down to smoke y'all out.

GEORGE

Very much appreciated.

(JORDAN sparks the blunt and begins the rotation.)

JORDAN

So, what y'all been gettin into?

RON

Talkin bout hella life shit. Like, we boutta graduate. Shit's crazy.

JORDAN

Man, y'all should be excited. School sucks. Like, work sucks too, but at least you get paid, and like, I fuck with just havin to worry about when I got a shift. Whenever I don't, I'm just chillin.

CLYDE

Aren't you goin to community college next semester though?

JORDAN

Yeah. I'm tryna like get somethin vocational. I think I might be an electrician.

RON

That shit's a lotta math.

JORDAN

Yeah. Imma def need some adderall. But shit, like, how *are* y'all feelin bout graduatin?

GEORGE

Shit dude, I was sayin this right as you walked in, but like, imma be straight, cause imma have this degree, so like I def think I can fall back on something if I have to, but like, I'm not gonna, cause this music shit's life ya know? Like, I have to do it. Nothing else I really wanna do instead.

JORDAN

That's wassup. What bout you Clyde? You been thinkin bout that post grad life?

CLYDE

Shit, like, yeah I been thinkin, but I don't know. It'd be dope to like, use this bio degree to do somethin for the environment. I'd love to be helpin with my job. But, at the same time, I'd love to take time for myself after school and just fuck off somewhere pretty for a while.

RON

Gah damn dude I feel that. Like, I'd love to be makin a difference with what I'm doin. But, I don't know if my passion really aligns with that.

CLYDE

You don't think writin makes a difference?

RON

I like to think it does. I know it helps build community, and that's dope. But like, it mostly builds a community of writers, and that shit can just, like feel like an echo chamber. Also, I feel like the shit I write is more for me than other people, so... I don't know.

GEORGE

But see that's important. Artists create for themselves for sure. Like I said, I make music 'cause I have to. But, if you put yourself into the world through your art and people connect to that, even if that connection is only helpin someone get through an hour of boredom, that means somethin. That's makin a difference. Like you said, that's buildin community.

                              RON

Yeah. Maybe. But…

                    (JORDAN exhales blunt smoke.)

                            JORDAN

But what?

                              RON

Just like… y'all are both talkin bout how you gotta do what you love and that'll fix the world and… I just don't know if I believe that.

                            GEORGE

But, how is you being miserable gonna help anything?

                              RON

By like, sacrificing my happiness for the greater good.

                            GEORGE

By doing what?

                              RON

I don't know, like going into politics or something.

                            JORDAN

Politics ain't shit.

                            GEORGE

I can agree with that.

                            CLYDE

Nah, like, I'm with you Ron. I think about that shit a lot. Like, maybe I need to stop thinking bout workin towards a passion and start workin towards… I don't know something with more utility.

                            JORDAN

Isn't your passion pretty utile?

RON

Is utile a word?

JORDAN

Shhh. It is. But, shhh. Clyde please go ahead.

CLYDE

Well, I don't know if my passion is utile or not because I don't really know what my passion is. I like ecology, and I think I could do good with it. But, I don't love it. But, I don't know how long it'll take me to figure out what I love, and I worry that's what's wrong with the world. Like, everyone's taking too much time tryna find what'll fulfill them rather than lookin for something they kinda enjoy that works to help everyone.

GEORGE

Nah I don't know dude. That sounds like how you end up resenting your life and wondering what could have been. That's how you end up like my parents. And they don't wanna help anyone. If you resent your life, you aren't gonna wanna help someone else's.

RON

I don't think either of us are talking about a situation where you resent your life.

GEORGE

But if you aren't chasing your dream or living your dream, how you keep yourself from going jaded?

JORDAN

Shit man, I got no fuckin clue. That's why I'm just out here doin me and hopin for the best.

CLYDE

You don't ever feel like you should do more?

JORDAN

What more ya gonna do? If you happy with yourself, you put good energy out to everyone else. That shit's contagious. Not all lovely people love themselves, but I'm positive all the dicks sure don't.

                          CLYDE
So your plan to fix all the world's problems is to just… vibe?

                          JORDAN
You got a better plan?

                          CLYDE
I'm figuring one out.

                          JORDAN
Then don't come at me. 'Cause I got my shit figured out, and my shit's
been workin'.

                          GEORGE
Gah damn. I love this motherfucker.

                          JORDAN
Back at ya homie.

                          RON
Wait, wait. Watcha mean by your shit's been workin?

                          JORDAN
Just like, my good vibe's been bringin others good vibes. So it's just
like, all good vibes.

                          RON
How much you smoked today?

                          JORDAN
Nah nah nah. You're not getting it.

                          GEORGE
He's not gettin it.

                          JORDAN
He's not gettin it. Ron, you're not gettin it.

            (RON waits for JORDAN to explain. JORDAN
            doesn't.)

RON

How am I not gettin it?

JORDAN

Like, you just gotta love and put that shit out in the world, whether that be through music,

(He gestures to GEORGE.)

through writing,

(He gestures to RON.)

Or through like… figurin out what brings you love.

(He gestures to CLYDE.)

Throw that love out to the universe and the universe gonna give that to someone who needs it.

CLYDE

That's a beautiful thought.

JORDAN

That's a beautiful truth.

RON

I hope so.

(JORDAN makes a gesture to say, "you can keep your doubts. Agree to disagree.")

GEORGE

What you throwin out to the universe, Jordan?

JORDAN

Man, everything. I'm not creatin or nothin. But, I got love for my life, so I guess I'm just throwin my life out to the universe. What's gonna happen's gonna happen.

RON

You believe in fate?

JORDAN

I believe there's a lotta shit in motion outside of our control.

RON

That don't scare you?

JORDAN

Sometimes it does, but I try not to worry bout it most of the time. Like
I said, I'm just tryna do me. Live my life to the best of my ability, and
believe that that's gonna work out.

RON

But, like, what about long term?

JORDAN

I'm boutta be an electrician. That's all the long term I got. But, also I
don't know if I wanna be an electrician. That may not be long term.

RON

So, no long term?

JORDAN

You got a long term?

RON

I mean you've heard the possibilities I got in my head..

JORDAN

Shit, man, then you got less of a long term than me.

GEORGE

Ron's spending so much time worryin about multiple long terms that
both might pass him by.

RON

Man fuck off. It's hard not to worry. It's a challenge to go into a world
that's not falling apart and this one is.

JORDAN

But dude, I've been in the world and like, I've met hella good people tryin their best so like, I really think the world's gonna be okay.

GEORGE

And even if it isn't, what're you gonna do?

JORDAN

But like it prolly will.

GEORGE

I admire the outlook.

JORDAN

What's the point in thinkin the world will end?

GEORGE

So you ain't surprised when it does.

JORDAN

Fair enough. But, I like livin my life surprised. I prefer to walk through the world bein like, "oh so this is happenin now? Bet. Let's go."

GEORGE

Huh. I live life bein like, "oh so this is happenin now? I fuckin knew it."

CLYDE

I like livin life bein like, "oh so this is happenin now? Do I wanna be a part of this?" If I decide nah then I dip.

RON

And I live life bein like, "oh so this is happenin now? When the hell did this start happening? I guess this is my life now."

GEORGE

'Cause you spendin all your time worrying about saving a world that you don't have the means to save.

CLYDE

Ain't nothin wrong with wanting to save the world.

GEORGE

But neither you or Ron actually wanna save the world, otherwise you'd be out there workin to save it. You want to wanna save the world, but you don't know what you want. Figure that out and then you can figure out how that's gonna help the world. That's what I'm doin.

RON

Is that what you're doin?

GEORGE

Damn straight. I know I want this music shit, so imma go get it. Then, once I got it, imma give some of it back.

CLYDE

Oh I got it. So, you think you're gonna be rich then?

GEORGE

I know so. Imma get this money, and that's how I'm gonna help the world.

RON

Bruh, I write poetry. That is not a lucrative business.

GEORGE

You also write songs. You know you could always commit to this music shit with me. I'd love to work together on this.

RON

Maybe I will.

JORDAN

Nah see that's your issue. Just do you dude! We coud all see that fuckin smirk in your eyes; it's obvious you love this music shit too. Just do it!

RON

I don't know man.

GEORGE

And I think you do. But hey, I'm not bringin anyone along who ain't ready to go all in. Think about it.

RON

Bet. I got you.

GEORGE

But don't think about it too long now. I'm planning moves before senior year's done.

RON

Okay.

CLYDE

Yeah that's all dope and what not. But what about those of us who have no apparent passions?

JORDAN

Bruh, how many times I gotta say this? Do you!

CLYDE

The fuck does that even mean right now Jordan?

JORDAN

Dog, I don't got any apparent passions either. My big goal right now is to maybe be an electrician, but I ain't worried. Why? 'Cause I'm doin me. I'm figuring me out.

CLYDE

But how does that do anything for the greater good?

JORDAN

I already told you dude. Because I ain't worryin, I got plenty more time to put out love into the world, more time to be kind to my fellow man and all that. 'Cause, y'all, imma say it one more time for those in the back, what more are we gonna do? We don't got funds yet. We don't got a platform. All we got is those around us, so let's love those folks and hope they pass it on and hope that it all just keeps gettin passed on and does somethin.

CLYDE

But what if that's not enough?

GEORGE

Unless we start runnin shit, nothin will be enough. We do what we can. And if we can't do that, we try to.

CLYDE

Maybe my passion is doing enough.

GEORGE

Then maybe you oughta run for office.

JORDAN

Aw shit. President Clyde.

RON

I'd vote for you.

GEORGE

I would too. And I don't vote.

RON

Wait, bruh, you don't vote?

GEORGE

Ain't never been a politician worth voting for.

RON

But like don't you want to at least have a say in who runs shit?

GEORGE

We don't have a say in who runs shit. We don't vote for the ultra fuckin wealthy that run this country.

RON

But we can vote for someone who ain't gonna listen to those fucks.

GEORGE

Let me know when you find 'em.

RON

Fair enough. But, like you could still vote for someone who's gonna listen to the less harmful of the ultra wealthy fucks.

GEORGE

Why? That's just reinforcing a broken system.

RON

But at least you're trying to keep the broken system from stabbing you in the gut too much.

GEORGE

You're still getting stabbed.

RON

But it's better to get stabbed less.

GEORGE

I just don't wanna get stabbed.

RON

Okay, but you're getting stabbed no matter what.

GEORGE

Exactly.

RON

But, if you don't vote you're just letting someone stab you more.

GEORGE

And if you do vote, you're asking someone to stab you.

RON

Clyde, you vote right?

CLYDE

Dude, I'm the one who's thinking about going into politics right now. Yes, I vote.

RON

Jordan?

JORDAN

Eh...

RON

Eh?

JORDAN

I don't know... I see what you're both sayin, but like... it's so much work to get out and vote, and my polling station is right by the police station, so like, yikes. I'm just like why put in that work when I ain't even passionate about who I'm voting for.

RON

So like, you think you'd vote if it was easier?

JORDAN

I'd be way more likely to.

RON

See this is why voting should be easier! George, you think you'd vote if it was easier?

GEORGE

Nah, it's the principal for me.

RON

I guess I can respect you for sticking to your principals. Even if they're trash.

(GEORGE flips RON off and they all laugh.)

RON

Ugh y'all. Why does shit always have obstacles?

GEORGE

If shit came easy, it'd all be crap.

CLYDE

That's fuckin bars dude.

JORDAN

Hmmm… but like if the path you're on don't make you wanna beat the shit out some obstacles maybe you gotta just go off in the woods and camp.

CLYDE

Bruh, fuckin *bars*. Y'all're spittin facts.

GEORGE

Don't do nothin else.

JORDAN

It's like with my ex. Y'all remember Kira right?

GEORGE

Yeah.

RON

We remember Kira.

CLYDE

Fuckin' Kira man.

JORDAN

Bet. So like, we dated for a long time-

CLYDE

Too long.

JORDAN

Hey, no regrets.

CLYDE

Dude, that shit nearly wrecked all of us. You still don't talk to Nate.

JORDAN

That's on Nate.

RON

I think he misses you dude.

JORDAN

I don't miss him.

RON

I don't know, might be worth reachin out.

JORDAN

Nah see, that's what I'm sayin. I didn't fuck with the path enough for the obstacle. So, I didn't try to fix shit with Nate, and definitely not Kira. I chose to camp in the woods with y'all. These woods are sick. Y'all are stellar trees.

CLYDE

Thanks man.

GEORGE

I fuck with trees.

RON

Trees are dope as hell. But like, Jordan, you ever worry about what happened to Nate when you left that path?

JORDAN

No regrets dude. Just choices.

CLYDE

BARS again! George when is the mixtape coming?

GEORGE

Just finished recordin the last song yesterday, just gotta mix and master.

CLYDE

You get J on that shit?

GEORGE

Not this time, but all y'all welcome to drop some heat.

JORDAN/CLYDE

Bet.

JORDAN

But yeah, if I chose to walk away, I had a good reason, and I trust that shit.

RON

Y'all think this country's a path worth its obstacles?

CLYDE

I think it could be. I feel like it's a country built off of potential. Just never reached it yet.

GEORGE

My whole life's here. That's worth the obstacles.

JORDAN

Plenty of woods to camp in here.

RON

Yeah… yeah. Just all of that… yeah.

(They sit in silence.)

RON

Y'all think we're still gonna hang once school's done?

GEORGE

We have so far. Why stop now?

RON

I don't know. We've always had this as our place to come back to. That's gonna change once we all go off and do our own things.

GEORGE

You and me may not be goin separate ways Ron. If you get your head outta your ass.

(RON laughs.)

                            RON
Man fuck off, I already said I'd think about it. I mean that.

                            CLYDE
I don't know man. I think we'll pick a new spot. We can all crash at one
of our apartments or somethin.

                            RON
I could dig that.

                            JORDAN
Y'all better be prepared for me to show up very unannounced, with a
blunt, or two, or six.

                            RON
Like a weed fairy.

                            JORDAN
I prefer weed Oprah. You get a blunt! You get a blunt! You get a blunt!

                            RON
Have you even watched Oprah?

                            JORDAN
Not once.

                    (They laugh.)

                            GEORGE
Yeah y'all, this is it. Like, if we've made it through all this, we're homies
for life. No matter what, we gon hang. I'll be like 35 and have like kids
and shit, but, you know I'm still gon be down to kick it like this.

                            CLYDE
Same.

                            RON
Yeah. Same.

JORDAN

Same. Minus the kids.

RON

Well bet. Smokin and talkin nonsense for life. As long as the world doesn't end first.

JORDAN

Nah man, I'm tellin you the world's gonna be just fine.

GEORGE

And even if it isn't…

(They all let that trail off and stare at the stars.)

BLACKOUT